GOSPEL SHAPED

WORK

Handbook

GOSPEL SHAPED

Tom Nelson

 THE GOSPEL
COALITION

thegoodbook
COMPANY

Gospel Shaped Work Handbook
© The Gospel Coalition / The Good Book Company 2016

Published by:
The Good Book Company
Tel (US): 866 244 2165
Tel (UK): 0333 123 0880
Email (US): info@thegoodbook.com
Email (UK): info@thegoodbook.co.uk

Websites:
North America: www.thegoodbook.com
UK: www.thegoodbook.co.uk
Australia: www.thegoodbook.com.au
New Zealand: www.thegoodbook.co.nz

ISBN: 9781909919242 Printed in the US

PRODUCTION TEAM:

AUTHOR:
Tom Nelson

**SERIES EDITOR FOR
THE GOSPEL COALITION:**
Collin Hansen

**SERIES EDITOR FOR
THE GOOD BOOK COMPANY:**
Tim Thornborough

**MAIN TEACHING SESSION
DISCUSSIONS:** Alison Mitchell

DAILY DEVOTIONALS:
Carl Laferton

BIBLE STUDIES:
Tim Thornborough

EDITORIAL ASSISTANTS:
Jeff Robinson (TGC), Rachel Jones (TGBC)

VIDEO EDITOR:
Phil Grout

PROJECT ADMINISTRATOR:
Jackie Moralee

EXECUTIVE PRODUCER:
Brad Byrd

DESIGN:
André Parker

# CONTENTS

 **PREFACE**

GROWING A GOSPEL SHAPED CHURCH

The Gospel Coalition is a group of pastors and churches in the Reformed heritage who delight in the truth and power of the gospel, and who want the gospel of Christ crucified and resurrected to lie at the center of all we cherish, preach and teach.

We want churches called into existence by the gospel to be shaped by the gospel in their everyday life.

Through our fellowship, conferences, and online and printed media, we have sought to encourage pastors and church leaders to calibrate their lives around what is of first importance—the gospel of Christ. In these resources, we want to provide those same pastors with the tools to excite and equip church members with this mindset.

In our foundation documents, we identified five areas that should mark the lives of believers in a local fellowship:

1. Empowered corporate worship
2. Evangelistic effectiveness
3. Counter-cultural community
4. The integration of faith and work
5. The doing of justice and mercy

We believe that a church utterly committed to winsome and theologically substantial expository preaching, and that lives out the gospel in these areas, will display its commitment to dynamic evangelism, apologetics, and church planting. These gospel-shaped churches will emphasize repentance, personal renewal, holiness, and the wonderful life of the church as the body of Christ. At the same time, there will be engagement with the social structures of ordinary people, and cultural engagement with art, business, scholarship and government. The church will be characterized by firm devotion to the truth on the one hand, and by transparent compassion on the other.

The Gospel Coalition believes in the priority of the local church, and that the local church is the best place to discuss these five ministry drivers and decide how to integrate them into life and mission. So, while being clear on the biblical principles, these resources give space to consider what a genuine expression of a gospel-shaped church looks like for you in the place where God has put you, and with the people he has gathered into fellowship with you.

Through formal teaching sessions, daily Bible devotionals, group Bible studies and the regular preaching ministry, it is our hope and prayer that congregations will grow into maturity, and so honor and glorify our great God and Savior.

Don Carson
President

Tim Keller
Vice President

INTRODUCTION

As gospel-loving people, we say that the gospel influences every dimension of our lives; yet many of us struggle with living out a gospel-shaped faith, particularly when it comes to our work. It is easy and convenient to compartmentalize our lives, worshiping one way on Sunday and working in quite another way on Monday. Are your Sunday faith and your Monday work seemingly worlds apart? Is your Christian faith speaking into what you do in the majority of your life? Are you experiencing a sizeable Sunday to Monday gap? I have good news. God's design and desire for you is to embrace a gospel-shaped faith that closes the gap between your Sunday worship and your Monday work.

The Gospel Coalition is addressing the importance of narrowing the all too common Sunday to Monday gap in their Theological Vision for Ministry, entitled, The Integration of Faith and Work:

> *Christians glorify God not only through the ministry of the Word, but also through their vocations of agriculture, art, business, government, scholarship— all for God's glory and the furtherance of the public good. Too many Christians have learned to seal off their faith-beliefs from the way they work in their vocation. The gospel is seen as a means of finding individual peace and not as the foundation of a worldview—a comprehensive interpretation of reality affecting all that we do. But we have a vision for a church that equips its people to think out the implications of the gospel on how we do carpentry, plumbing, data-entry, nursing, art, business, government, journalism, entertainment, and scholarship. Such a church will not only support Christians' engagement with culture, but will also help them work with distinctiveness, excellence, and accountability in their trades and professions...*[1]

In this curricular journey of exploration, we will address both theologically and practically the Sunday to Monday gap. We desire to guide you to greater understanding of how a more integral Christian faith shapes you as a worker, informs the work you do and influences the workplace you inhabit. In each session you will encounter life-changing truths flowing from Holy Scripture regarding the paid or unpaid work you are called to do throughout the week. You will become aware in fresh and transforming ways of how you have been created

---

1 You can read the full text of the statement on page 176 of this Handbook.

and redeemed with work in mind. Your mind will be challenged and your heart encouraged with a hopeful realism, remembering that the work you do now in this time of redemptive history is both energizing and agonizing, both fulfilling and frustrating. You can anticipate a renewed sense of joy from knowing more fully the biblical truth that one day yet future, you will work without the thorns and thistles that are now an inescapable part of the brokenness of all work. In the mysterious providence of God, you will discover it is in and through the joys and pains of your work that you are called to worship God, be spiritually formed, love your neighbors, live out the gospel and proclaim the gospel to others.

It is my heartfelt and hopeful prayer that as you work through this curriculum, you will increasingly realize how much the gospel speaks into the work you are called to do each and every day. May you gain a greater glimpse of how very much your work matters to God and to others, and may the inspired words of the apostle Paul grace your journey of discovery! "Whatever you do, work heartily, as for the Lord and not for men, knowing that from the Lord you will receive the inheritance as your reward. You are serving the Lord Christ" (Colossians 3:23-24).

Tom Nelson

HOW TO USE GOSPEL SHAPED WORK

MAIN TEACHING SESSION This session combines watching short talks on a DVD or listening to "live" talks with times for discussion. These prompt you to think about what you have heard and how it might apply to your church and cultural context. Bear in mind that there is not necessarily a "right answer" to every question!

DEVOTIONALS Each session comes with six daily personal devotionals. These look at passages that are linked to the theme of the Main Teaching Session, and are for you to read and meditate on at home through the week after the session. You may like to do them in addition to or instead of your usual daily devotionals, or use them to begin such a practice.

JOURNAL As you reflect on what you have learned as a group and in your personal devotionals, use this page to record the main truths that have struck you, things you need to pray about, and issues you'd like to discuss further or questions you'd like to ask.

BIBLE STUDY As part of this curriculum, your church may be running weekly Bible Studies as well as the Main Teaching Sessions. These look more closely at a passage and help you focus on an aspect of the Main Teaching Session. If your church is not using this part of the curriculum, you could work through it on your own or with another church member.

SERMON NOTES Your church's preaching program may be following this curriculum; space has been provided for you to make notes on these sermons in your Handbook.

SESSION 1:

CREATED TO
WORK

WHY ARE WE HERE? THAT IS OFTEN A SURPRISINGLY DIFFICULT QUESTION TO ANSWER – AND NOT MANY OF US WOULD INCLUDE THE WORD "WORK" IN OUR RESPONSE. IN THIS SESSION, WE'LL DISCOVER THAT ONE OF THE PURPOSES FOR WHICH WE WERE CREATED IS, IN FACT, TO WORK – AND WHY THAT IS SUCH WONDERFUL NEWS.

CREATED TO WORK

Discuss

If you went out on the street and asked people the question "Why are we here?" what answers do you think you might get?

▶ WATCH DVD 1.1 OR LISTEN TO TALK 1.1

Discuss

 READ GENESIS 1:26 – 2:3

²⁶ Then God said, "Let us make man in our image, after our likeness. And let them have dominion over the fish of the sea and over the birds of the heavens and over the livestock and over all the earth and over every creeping thing that creeps on the earth."

²⁷ So God created man in his own image,

> in the image of God he created him;

> male and female he created them.

²⁸ And God blessed them. And God said to them, "Be fruitful and multiply and fill the earth and subdue it, and have dominion over the fish of the sea and over the birds of the heavens and over every living thing that moves on the earth." ²⁹ And God said, "Behold, I have given you every plant yielding seed that is on the face of all the earth, and every tree with seed in its fruit. You shall have them for food. ³⁰ And to every beast of the earth and to every bird of the heavens and to everything that creeps on the earth, everything that has the breath of life, I have given every green plant for food." And it was so. ³¹ And God saw everything that he had made, and behold, it was very good. And there was evening and there was morning, the sixth day.

2 Thus the heavens and the earth were finished, and all the host of them. ² And on the seventh day God finished his work that he had done, and he rested on the seventh day from all his work that he had done. ³ So God blessed the seventh day and made it holy, because on it God rested from all his work that he had done in creation.

In Genesis 1:28, God tells the first people how they are to live. What are the five commands he gives them, and what do they mean?

How does this help to answer our opening question: "Why are we here?"

Genesis 2:3 tells us that God is a worker. We can also discern one of the reasons why he works—he loves his creation and wants to bless it. He created us in his image (Genesis 1:27), so *all* humans—as his image bearers—are created to be workers too. Does the idea that you were made to be a worker surprise you? What difference might this truth make on your journey to work, or as you start your day?

▶ **WATCH DVD 1.2 OR LISTEN TO TALK 1.2**

Discuss

In this curriculum, we will see that work is more than just what we do each day, or how we pay our way. Work is creation, collaboration and cultivation—whatever our daily occupation, paid or not.

Look at your work (paid or otherwise) through the lens of "work as creation." How does your specific work help to build, create, strengthen or expand human society?

Work is primarily cultivation—contributing something to the world. But it is also collaboration in two ways: collaboration with God, and collaboration with each other. Can you see how the work you do (paid or otherwise) is collaboration in one or both of these ways?

Work as cultivation means that we are to grow and steward the raw materials of creation. How does your work take the "raw materials" of God's creation to enhance the lives of others?

▶ **WATCH DVD 1.3 OR LISTEN TO TALK 1.3**

Discuss

"There is no such thing as menial labor." How does this change the way you think about dull tasks you undertake during the day, and/or about people who do the kinds of jobs your society considers "menial"?

As we think about work over the next few weeks, what questions about work are you hoping will be answered?

Pray

Genesis 1 says that we are created to work and that work is fundamentally good.

Pray that during the course of this curriculum, God will show you any attitudes to work that need to change.

Pray that you will grow as godly workers, who are images of God to the world around you.

DAILY BIBLE DEVOTIONALS

These six devotionals focus on Psalm 8, a hymn of praise enjoying the truths of Genesis 1 – 2. We see who God is and who we are—and whose we are, and why we are here.

Day 1

PSALM 8:1

Q: *What is the whole earth intended to show us?*

Q: *What are all the "heavens" above us intended to show us?*

Every single aspect of the creation points to its Creator. A snowflake's intricacy… a lightning bolt's power… a cell's complexity… a sunset's beauty. Each tells us there is a Maker, and each tells us something of the Maker. We see his glory reflected in each part of his work that we see around us. And, just as walking through a medieval monarch's palace was intended to drive you to your knees by the time you reached his throneroom, so creation is designed to cause us to worship the Lord in awe, as heaven does: **read Revelation 4:11**.

As we look up at our Majesty from our knees, we are in the right—the only—position to appreciate that God is not only *the* Lord, but *our* Lord. He is the God of all things, who reveals himself personally to his people. Wherever you go today, at work and at rest, in the good and the hard, remember: *I know the God who runs this place.*

PRAY: *O LORD, our Lord, how majestic is your name in all the earth!*

Day 2

PSALM 8:2

After the awe of v 1, this verse seems strange.

Q: *Does all of God's creation recognize that he is its rightful King?*

Q: *Where has God "established [his] strength"? Why is this a strange way to counter his "foes"?*

The truth written in poetry here was seen in history later when the One who molded the planets walked on earth—**read Matthew 21:12-17**. It was not the powerful who proclaimed the truth about the Son of God— God had "hidden these things from the wise and understanding and revealed them to little children" (Matthew 11:25). This points to a profound truth about the world's Maker: *The all-present, all-powerful One chooses to work through those who are small and weak.*

If you are feeling strong today, take care that you do not rely on yourself and oppose your Creator. If you know you are weak, take heart that you are just the kind of person through whom God displays his strength and achieves his purposes. **Read 2 Corinthians 12:7-10.**

PRAY: *Creator God, I am a frail creature. Let me see my weaknesses not as a disaster, but as an opportunity to showcase your glory.*

Day 3

PSALM 8:3-4

Q: *As we look into the sky on a clear night, what is one thing we should ask? How should we feel?*

Considering creation should not only cause us to magnify our view of the Creator, but prompt us to diminish our sense of ourselves. Look at another planet in our solar system—unreachable for mankind, yet just one of roughly 1 million billion billion planets crafted by God with a word. You and I really are small—tiny specks on a small rock in a far-flung corner of the universe.

Q: *How does considering creation—and both the One who made it and we who live in it—show us how ridiculous it is to:*
- *disobey God's commands?*
- *doubt God's power?*
- *deny God's authority over us?*

All of us have a god-complex—we tend to think we should call the shots in our lives, and that God should mold himself to fit our priorities and practices. Looking at creation is one way of helping ourselves to wrestle the crown off our own heads, so that we might gaze in wonder and gasp in awe: "How majestic is your name in all the earth" (v 1, 9).

Q: *When do you find it hardest to remember that God is God, and that you are not? How would remembering how many planets he has made, and how many you have made, help you?*

PRAY: *Creator God, help me to know my smallness, that I would magnify your greatness.*

Day 4

Only if we ask the question of verse 4 are we ready to appreciate the truth of verse 5…

PSALM 8:5

Q: *What position did God give humanity?*

Q: *Given who God is, and who we are, why is this an awesome truth?*

Yes, we are very, very small. But we are not inconsequential—not an afterthought in the great creating works of God. Quite the reverse: we were the pinnacle, given "glory and honor" as he made our first ancestors in his image (Genesis 1:26-28), able to relate to him and able to reflect him.

We are not mere specks, because we are cared-for creatures, given the privileged position of knowing God. The tragedy is that, because we do not like to be dependent upon or subject to anyone, we tend to reject our created-ness. And that relegates us to mere matter, which does not matter much. The paradoxical truth is that it is only as we embrace our smallness that we can glimpse our greatness—a greatness that comes not from being independent self-rulers, but from being dependent creatures made by God and fashioned in his image.

Q: *How do verse 4 and verse 5 help you see yourself neither too highly, nor too lowly?*

Q: *How might v 4-5 be a helpful way into talking to a skeptic about the gospel?*

PRAY: *Lord, enable me to live with a sense of humility because I am a creature; and of dignity because I am made in your image.*

Day 5

PSALM 8:6-9

Verse 5 showed us that as humans we have a God-given dignity…

Q: *What does verse 6 say God has given us?*

Q: *How should this verse affect the way we view our work, whether it is in the home, the factory, the field or the office?*

Don't miss how astonishing it is that God made us not only to relate to him and reflect him, but to *rule* under him. He invites us to share in his plans for his world, so that we might stand with him in eternity and say not only, "*He did that*" but, "*We did that.*"

Q: *How does remembering that we rule over the works of God's hands, and not ours, affect how we use the power we have?*

Things go wrong with our work in the world when we forget one of two things. First, that in some smaller or larger way, each of us has been given *dominion*—what we do matters, and our work can (and should) make a difference. Second, that we have been *given* dominion—it is delegated by God, and we are accountable to God. Our dominion must never be exercised in a way that seeks to defy his purposes, or to trample on his commands.

Q: *How do verses 6-8 help you to go to work (or stay home to work) with purpose and joy today?*

PRAY: *Lord, thank you for calling me to contribute to the furthering of your plans. Help me to connect my daily work to your purposes in this world.*

Day 6

Psalm 8 tells us so much about ourselves—and yet it is not really about us at all…

HEBREWS 2:5-10

Q: *Having quoted Psalm 8, what does this writer to first-century Christians remind them that God did (middle of v 8)?*

Q: *But what do we not see (end of v 8)?*

We love to have dominion… but we want it independently, for we do not love to have dominion under God, used in line with his commands. In trying to rule without God, we forfeit the ability to rule the world under God. There is a great mismatch between what Psalm 8 says about the earth, and what we see on the earth. We do not relate to God rightly, reflect God clearly, or rule under God properly.

Q: *But what do we "see" (v 9)?*

There is a perfect human, who came from heaven and was made lower than the angels, who exercized his dominion humbly and perfectly, and who died for his people to restore their relationship to God. We see this man—"namely Jesus" (v 9)—crowned with glory and honor. Jesus will rule "the world to come" (v 5), and so we look forward to him restoring us, as "sons" of God (v 10), to be the people we were created to be, working and ruling alongside him in his recreated world.

Q: *Re-read Psalm 8 as a song about Jesus. How does this increase your praise of our Lord, "majestic … in all the earth"?*

PRAY: *Memorize Psalm 8. Meditate on it. Pray you would live, and work, in light of it.*

JOURNAL

What I've learned or been particularly struck by this week…

What I want to change in my perspectives or actions as a result of this week…

Things I would like to think about more or discuss with others at my church…

BIBLE STUDY

Discuss

When the subject of work comes up in conversation, what kinds of attitudes do people show toward work? Is that range of attitudes the same when you discuss work at church with other Christians?

This first session of *Gospel Shaped Work* has shown us some big ideas that may be unfamiliar to people.

- How does the Bible first reveal God? As a worker who loves his job!

- Why are we here? God created us to work!

- What is God's "Creation Mandate" for the world? For humans made in God's image to fill the earth and subdue it.

- How are we to fulfill that command? By creating, co-operating and cultivation.

Let's understand these fundamental truths more deeply as we look again at Genesis 1.

☞ READ GENESIS 1:1-25

> [20] And God said, "Let the waters swarm with swarms of living creatures, and let birds fly above the earth across the expanse of the heavens." [21] So God created the great sea creatures and every living creature that moves, with which the waters swarm, according to their kinds, and every winged bird according to its kind. And God saw that it was good.

1. After God made the heavens and the earth (v 1), what was the earth like (v 2)?

2. From verse 3 onwards we see God at work. What do we learn about the kind of worker God is from these verses?

3. If you look at creation, what does it tell us about our Creator (see also Romans 1 v 19-20)?

READ GENESIS 1:26-31

> 26 Then God said, "Let us make man in our image, after our likeness. And let them have dominion over the fish of the sea and over the birds of the heavens and over the livestock and over all the earth and over every creeping thing that creeps on the earth."

4. We are "made in the image of God" (v 27)—who is revealed as a worker in Genesis 1. Go through each of your answers to question 2—which of these aspects of God's character do you see in your own work? Which are you best at? Where might you need to develop?

5. What are the five commands God gives to the whole of humankind in verse 28? How can we see the human race fulfill these commands in general? How can you see aspects of them in the work that you do?

6. How should these truths about our nature and position as people in God's world affect the way we view ourselves? How might it change the way we see others?

7. Think about how you feel as you start work on a Monday morning. Think about common attitudes to work among your friends and colleagues. How might the perspective of Genesis 1 change our view of work—whatever that might be?

8. Think of some practical ways we can honor those who work around us—especially those whose work is often considered routine or "low grade."

Apply

FOR YOURSELF: Do you need to change your fundamental attitude toward work? Have you been guilty of a downbeat attitude toward it that does not honor God? How will you help yourself to think differently about work this week?

FOR YOUR CHURCH: Is talking about work subtly looked down on in your church, as if it is not a fit subject for conversation? How often is work referred to in a positive and constructive way in sermons, Bible studies and other church meetings? How might you cultivate a more positive way to discuss work, and work-related matters in the life of your church?

Pray

FOR YOUR GROUP: Discover what each member of your group actually does work wise. Today, try not to focus on particular problems or difficulties—we will get to that next time!. Instead, give thanks for the work, and the way it contributes to God's creation commands.

FOR YOUR CHURCH: As your church embarks on this series examining what it means to let the gospel shape the way we think about work, pray that you would grow together in seeing more clearly the Lord Jesus Christ, and his perfect work in saving us.

SERMON NOTES

Bible passage: Date:

SESSION 2:
WORK AND THE FALL

SINCE WE WERE DESIGNED TO KNOW THE JOY OF WORK IN GOD'S CREATION, WHY DO OUR WORKING LIVES OFTEN HAVE AS MUCH FRUSTRATION IN THEM AS THEY DO FULFILLMENT? THIS SESSION WILL SHOW US HOW TO BE REALISTIC ABOUT OUR WORK, WITHOUT BEING WITHOUT HOPE IN OUR WORK.

WORK AND THE FALL

Discuss

What is the most frustrating thing about your daily occupation?

READ GENESIS 3:1-19

> [1] Now the serpent was more crafty than any other beast of the field that the Lord God had made...

WATCH DVD 2.1 OR LISTEN TO TALK 2.1

Discuss

In Session 1 we saw that work is creation, collaboration and cultivation. But, because of sin, work is no longer what it could and should be. Can you think of examples of the following?

• Work as broken creation

• Work as broken collaboration

• Work as broken cultivation

"Seasons of fruitfulness are often quickly consumed by times of hardship." Have you experienced this yourself, or seen it happen elsewhere?

▶ WATCH DVD 2.2 OR LISTEN TO TALK 2.2

Discuss

"We are not simply victims of the brokenness of our workplace; we are co-conspirators." Can you think of examples from your own job or daily occupation where your sin has had a negative impact on your work or on those you work with?

We should not be surprised that work is marred by the results of the fall. But as Christians we will want to act in a way that honors God. How might a Christian respond to the following?

- A co-worker who regularly tells inappropriate jokes
- A manager who bullies their staff
- A colleague who encourages you to work less hard so that you don't "show the rest of us up"
- A client who objects to you mentioning your faith

▶ WATCH DVD 2.3 OR LISTEN TO TALK 2.3

Discuss

How does Genesis 3 help you understand the frustrations of your workplace?

How might Genesis 3 give you hope as you face the frustrations of your work?

Pray

"We are not simply victims of the brokenness of our workplace; we are co-conspirators."

Ask God to forgive you for the times when you have contributed to the brokenness of your workplace. Ask him to help you to change. Ask him too, to help you to apologize and repent to a co-worker if that's needed.

Pray that you will be a light in your workplace, living in such a way that it both pleases God and points people to him.

DAILY BIBLE DEVOTIONALS

From chapter 3 onwards, Genesis reveals the effects of the fall on each generation. None of these episodes are primarily focused on work; yet all speak about work.

Day 1

GENESIS 4:1-16: CAIN & ABEL

Abel's offering (v 4) was the very best he had—the fat portions of the firstborn. Perhaps this is why God "had regard" for Abel's, but not Cain's (v 4-5). But the focus is not on Cain's offering so much as Cain's response.

Q: *How does Cain react, and what does God warn him of (v 5-7)?*

Q: *Does Cain heed the warning (v 8)?*

So the first human blood is spilled (v 10)—the first homicide; the first fratricide, in fact. The breaking of humans' relationship with God in one generation brings the breaking of their relationship with each other in the next.

Why did Cain kill Abel? Because he forfeited an acceptance he craved… grew envious and angry instead of repentant… and refused to close the door on sin, instead inviting it in. Cain killed Abel in his heart before he killed him in the field. Anger tends to spill over.

Q: *How have you seen this process in the workplace, and with what results?*

Q: *How have you seen this happen in your own heart and life, and with what results?*

PRAY: *Pray against envious anger. Thank God that, in Christ, you are already accepted by the only One who eternally matters.*

Day 2

GENESIS 4:17-24: LAMECH

Q: *How does Lamech appear to treat his wives (v 23)?*

Q: *How does he treat those who cross him (v 23-24)?*

Lamech is Cain's great-great-great-grandson; and he resembles him in his conduct. But where Cain tried to hide his crime, and then recognized it deserved God's punishment (v 9, 13-14), Lamech simply boasts of his conduct. His tone is one of pride, not of regret.

This is what sin does: it not only severs relationships; it sears the conscience as it celebrates itself. What would have been unthinkable in one generation becomes reality in the next, and promoted in the one after. **Read Romans 1:28-32.** Lamech's family are a picture of the paradox of fallen humanity: capable of cultivation (v 20) and creativity (v 21-22); yet equally responsible for great vengefulness and violence (v 23-24).

Q: *How have you seen sin accepted, and even celebrated, in the workplace?*

Q: *Are there any past working practices you need to repent of, or current workplace temptations you need to resist?*

PRAY: *Pray through your answer to that final question now.*

Day 3

Noah's story is well-known—apart from the last 10 verses. Here is what happened to the family God had rescued once they had left the ark to enjoy life in God's refreshed creation…

GENESIS 9:18-28: NOAH & HAM

Q: *What does Noah do with the fruit of his work in that refreshed creation (v 20-21)?*

Q: *In what state does his family end up (v 25-27)?*

Verse 22 is enigmatic. At the very least, Ham publicized the shame of his father lying naked in a drunken stupor. At the worst, "saw" means that Ham took advantage of his father's state to sexually assault him (as would happen again several generations later—19:30-38). The world had been renewed by the flood; but the human heart had not.

What was Noah doing? Using the fruit of his labors for his own self-gratification. Perhaps he was also spiritually complacent—his catastrophic sin follows his great act of obedience (building the ark) and God's great promise to him (the covenant). What was Ham doing? Exploiting a situation to his advantage, with no regard for another's reputation.

Q: *Self-gratification, spiritual complacency, exploitation… how do you see these effects of the fall in the workplace?*

Q: *How do you see them in your own heart?*

PRAY: *Confess times when you have fallen in these ways. Thank God that your salvation (like Noah's) relies on his promise, and not your performance.*

Day 4

GENESIS 11:1-9: BABEL

Q: *What do these people use their hard work and ingenuity to do (v 4)?*

Q: *What is their aim, positively and negatively (both are in v 4)?*

The motto of the builders is: "Let us" (v 3-4). But those are the words of God as he made humans—read 1:26. In building this tower, these creatures are grasping at the role of Creator. They have no need of God; they have themselves. And they are defying the rule of the Creator—he charged humans to "fill the earth" (1:28), but they build "lest we be dispersed over the face of the whole earth" (11:4). This is a self-reliant, self-promoting humanity, determined to construct a society built on the foundations of independence and ingenuity, rather than on God.

Q: *How does God's response both show the futility of their effort, and ensure that his plan for humanity is fulfilled (v 5-9)?*

Babel is a long way from Eden. There, humanity relied on God, was given greatness by God, and enjoyed fulfilling work under God. Now it is all about man; and it is all futile, because it is all frustrated. Perhaps Western workplaces are not far from Babel.

Q: *How are you tempted to work in a self-reliant, self-promoting way? How can you seek to serve and rely on God instead?*

PRAY: *Pray through the upcoming events of your day, seeking God's help to know and serve his purposes in every one of them.*

Day 5

God's response to Babel was judgment, but also promise. The builders had wanted to make their name great by defying God; God now promised one man that he would make his name great as he obeyed God (12:1-4). That man was the great, and flawed, Abram.

GENESIS 12:10-20: ABRAM

Q: *Given God's promise in v 1 and 7, what do you make of Abram's actions in v 10?*

Q: *Why does Abram tell Sarai to say she is his sister, instead of his wife (v 11-13)?*

Q: *What are the results of this deception (v 14-17)?*

Abram does what seems sensible, but not what is faithful (v 7). He acts to protect himself, not to promote truth; out of common sense, not out of a sense of God's trustworthiness. He has already learned that God keeps his promises (v 1, 7). But that is a lesson that is easily, and quickly, forgotten.

And so this man who was to be a blessing to others (v 2-3) becomes a curse to his host (v 17). Abram was a fallen man in a fallen world, and everything God achieved through him would be by grace.

Q: *In your own workplace, are you driven by a desire to protect yourself, or a desire to bless those around you?*

Q: *Why is living in explicit reliance on God's promises the best way to be a blessing?*

PRAY: *Ask God to help you to rely on his promises, and bless those around you.*

Day 6

The outworking of sin is one of the themes of Genesis; another is the blessing of living as a cared-for creature of the Creator. Today, we glimpse that attitude in a "workplace"…

GENESIS 24:1-28: THE SERVANT

Q: *What are the two things Abraham most cares about for his son Isaac (v 3-4, 5-6)?*

Abraham's concern is to ensure that he and his son obey the God who keeps his promises (v 7). Abraham has learned the greatest of all lessons: blessing is found in being ruled by and relying on God, even when it is hard.

Q: *How does the servant show his shared commitment to obeying God (v 9)?*

Q: *How does he show his reliance on God, both before and after his task is successful (v 12-14, 26-27)?*

Adam and Eve decided to rule and rely on themselves; we have traced sin's catastrophic effects, generation by generation. But here is a man who lives under God's rule and relies on him, asking for his help and praising him for his assistance. We do not know this man's name, but we do know he was a man of God.

Q: *When will it be hardest to live under God's rule and trust his promises in your work? See this as an opportunity!*

Q: *What do your prayers about your work suggest about who you rely on? Does anything need to change? How?*

PRAY: *Ask God to help you enjoy living under his rule, not your own, at work today.*

 **JOURNAL**

What I've learned or been particularly struck by this week…

What I want to change in my perspectives or actions as a result of this week…

Things I would like to think about more or discuss with others at my church…

BIBLE STUDY

Discuss

What do you love about your work? What kinds of things do you find frustrating or troubling?

We are all affected by the curse of the fall. In the well-known story that Jesus tells, and the teaching that follows, we can discern some false ways of thinking about work that easily influence our attitudes.

READ LUKE 12:13-21

> *15 Take care, and be on your guard against all covetousness, for one's life does not consist in the abundance of his possessions.*

1. What question prompts Jesus to tell his parable and why does he tell it (v 13-15)? What does Jesus see as the questioner's real problem?

2. Look at the details of the story in verses 16-19. What qualities does the man show that most people would applaud?

3. How would you sum up the man's attitude to work and rest? Can you come up with a couple of mottos that he might use to explain his approach to life?

4. What is his one big mistake? (Clue: What is repeated more than 10 times in v 17-19?) Why does it matter?

5. How can we can be infected by this way of thinking about our working lives. In what ways should we think differently to the world? What might it mean to be "rich toward God" in the way we think about work and retirement?

6. What other problems that flow from the fall can plague our working lives? Share with the group which of these you are most prone to, and discuss ways in which you can prevent yourself falling under their influence.

READ LUKE 12:22-34

> 22 *Therefore I tell you, do not be anxious about your life, what you will eat, nor about your body, what you will put on.*

7. How does the Lord Jesus go on to reassure those who love him as they live in this fallen world?

8. Which of these encouragements do you most need to hear today and why?

Apply

FOR YOURSELF: Think about your own attitude toward work in our fallen world. Which of these might God call "foolish"? What does wisdom look like? Is there something that needs to be thought through? Who will you do that with? How terrible for God to think you a fool because you look for identity and meaning in the wrong place.

FOR YOUR CHURCH: Do you honor and encourage others at your church in their work? Are you supporting and helping each other as you deal with the issues and problems you face at work? Are you encouraging each other to work hard, but to value Christ more? If you are a church leader, when was the last time work was mentioned as part of the application in a sermon?

Pray

FOR YOUR GROUP: Pray for the issues that people raised in question 6. Ask God to give you courage and wisdom—and the discernment to know when to apply each!

FOR YOUR CHURCH: Ask the Lord to help you support each other as a church in your work struggles and dilemmas. And pray that you would encourage others to find their identity and meaning in Christ, not work.

SERMON NOTES

Bible passage: Date:

SESSION 3:
RENEWED WORK

IT IS NOT ONLY PEOPLE THAT ARE BEING FREED FROM THE CONSEQUENCES OF SIN AND BROUGHT INTO FREEDOM AND THE PROMISE OF FUTURE RE-CREATION — IT IS THIS WORLD, TOO. AND THAT HAS PROFOUND CONSEQUENCES FOR HOW WE VIEW OUR WORK, WITH ALL ITS UPS AND DOWNS.

RENEWED WORK

▶ **WATCH DVD 3.1 OR LISTEN TO TALK 3.1**

Discuss

 **READ ROMANS 8:18-23**

> [18] For I consider that the sufferings of this present time are not worth comparing with the glory that is to be revealed to us. [19] For the creation waits with eager longing for the revealing of the sons of God. [20] For the creation was subjected to futility, not willingly, but because of him who subjected it, in hope [21] that the creation itself will be set free from its bondage to corruption and obtain the freedom of the glory of the children of God. [22] For we know that the whole creation has been groaning together in the pains of childbirth until now. [23] And not only the creation, but we ourselves, who have the firstfruits of the Spirit, groan inwardly as we wait eagerly for adoption as sons, the redemption of our bodies.

What are God's people, Christians, waiting eagerly for (v 23)?

How are God's people described in verses 19, 21 and 23? Why do you think this is?

What else will be redeemed and renewed (v 21-22)?

▶ WATCH DVD 3.2 OR LISTEN TO TALK 3.2

Discuss

"Work can either reshape us into the image of God or it can lead us into greater sin." Have you seen either or both of these things happening?

READ ROMANS 5:3-5

³ Not only that, but we rejoice in our sufferings, knowing that suffering produces endurance, ⁴ and endurance produces character, and character produces hope, ⁵ and hope does not put us to shame, because God's love has been poured into our hearts through the Holy Spirit who has been given to us.

In the DVD, Tom said: *"If we think suffering is bad and not from God, we will run away from it or grow bitter in it. But when we see it as coming from God's good hand, it can work in us to produce the priceless commodities of endurance, character and hope."* How does this shape your view of work when it is difficult, exhausting or unfair?

How might God be using your workplace to produce an endurance in you? How might he be using it to refocus your hope on him?

How did you respond to Tom's closing question: "Are you open to the possibility that God is seeking to use the frustrations and pain of your daily work to refocus our hopes around him?"

▶ WATCH DVD 3.3 OR LISTEN TO TALK 3.3

Discuss

Re-read Romans 8:19-22. As well as renewing people, God is in the business of renewing creation itself. How does Paul describe this process (v 22)? Why is this a good picture of what's happening to creation?

How will your own work (paid or otherwise) have lasting significance? How does your work create beauty, correct injustice, create peace, or lead to the flourishing of humanity?

_____

_____

_____

_____

Pray

Pray that God will remind you that "the sufferings of this present time are not worth comparing with the glory that is to be revealed to us" (Romans 8:18).

Ask God to enable to you to face the difficulties at work with faith, that they will reshape you into his image and refocus your hopes.

Thank God that one day the groaning, pain and futility of creation will be replaced by praise, healing and the restoration of his creation.

DAILY BIBLE DEVOTIONALS

Romans 8 shows us what is redeemed—people, and creation. Romans 1 – 5, which is our focus here, shows us why we need redemption, and how God achieved it.

Day 1

ROMANS 1:18-32

Q: *What is being "revealed" (1:18)? Why is this fair (v 19-21)?*

Q: *Paul lists sinful actions in v 24, 26b-27 and 29-32. What attitude lies behind all the actions (v 22-23, 25, 28)?*

We all worship something—either the Creator or something he created. And the heart loves to make a good, created thing into its god—its ultimate thing. By nature, we worship what is made, not what is immortal (v 23).

God's wrath is seen now in him giving us what we choose. Because we were made to know, worship and find fulfillment in serving the Creator, no created thing can fully or finally fulfill us or save us. And God's present judgment is to allow us to serve what will not satisfy us but instead enslaves us. He says: *This is what you have chosen; so this is what you will have.* The worst thing that can happen to someone is that God gives them what they want—because it can never give them what they need. Each of us needs redeeming—freeing—from our choosing to worship what is not God.

PRAY: *Confess how you treat good things as god things. Ask for help to honor and thank God, finding satisfaction in him.*

Day 2

Many people would respond to Romans 1:18-32 like this: *Yes, God should judge all those who don't worship him, and who live in those immoral ways. But I'm not like that. I seek to obey God.* But Paul isn't finished yet…

ROMANS 2:1-5

Q: *What happens whenever someone thinks they are right with God because they are morally better than someone else (v 1)?*

To "pass judgment" is to believe that others are worse than you, so they deserve God's judgment while you do not. It is salvation-by-comparison—and we find it very easy to do. We excuse our sin and magnify that of others, in order to convince ourselves that our goodness merits God's blessing or approval.

Q: *Do you ever think in this way?*

Q: *Since our judgment of others condemns us too, what lies ahead of us (v 5)?*

God's present judgment is to hand us over to worshiping good things, to a life rejecting his presence. God's future judgment is to take all good things away, in an eternity outside his presence. We need redeeming from our present wrong worship *and* our future hell.

PRAY: *Let God kindly lead you to repent of your efforts at salvation-by-comparison.*

Day 3

"None is righteous, no, not one..." (3:10). No one is in right standing with their Creator.

ROMANS 3:21-23

Q: *How has a way to be made right with God been "manifested" (v 21-22)? How does it not come (v 21)?*

Q: *How does someone take hold of this righteousness that God offers (v 22)?*

Q: *Why does everyone need it (v 22-23)?*

Outside the gospel, we stand or fall before God based on our own performance. We present our moral record to him and say: *Accept me.* As we've seen, that is a forlorn hope, since we have "fallen short" (v 23); our performance qualifies us for judgment, not for eternal life. *But now* God offers us perfect righteousness—his own righteousness—for us to accept from and present to him, so we can say with complete confidence: *Accept me.*

This perfect moral record is held out to us by Christ. It is not faith that saves, anymore than faith in my flapping arms to fly me across the Atlantic will save me. It is faith *in Jesus Christ* that saves. We do not have life now and life to come because of who we were, are, or will be, but because of who Christ is and what he did.

Q: *Do you believe? Have you ever reached out and taken the righteousness that God holds out to you through Jesus?*

PRAY: *Lord, my conduct leaves me deserving your rejection. I take hold of the righteousness you offer me in Christ. Thank you so, so much that you have made me acceptable to you.*

Day 4

ROMANS 3:22B-25A

To explain how we can be offered righteousness, Paul takes us on a tour of an ancient city.

First, we visit the lawcourt. We are guilty of sin, yet we are "justified by his grace" (v 24). "Justified" is a legal term for when a judge announces that the accused is not guilty, and is of good character. To be justified by God is not only not to face punishment; it is also to be praised; to move, spiritually speaking, from death row to receiving a Congressional Medal. And God does this "freely"—literally, without cause. It is his gift, not our merit.

Second, the slave market. We are justified "through the redemption that is in Christ Jesus" (v 24). We are enslaved to the things we worship (1:24-28) and trapped by our own sin, which leaves us facing judgment (2:5). To be freed from slavery, a price must be paid—a life. As Christ gave up his life, he paid that price, so that we might live free and unchained.

Third, the temple. God justifies and redeems us because God put Jesus "forward as a propitiation by his blood" (3:25). In the Old T, God's wrath was turned away from those who deserved it—was propitiated—through an animal's death. Ultimately, God's wrath is turned away from us because in the death of his Son, his wrath fell on his Son.

Q: *How does a sinner receive this wonderful status before God (end v 25a)?*

PRAY: *Picture yourself in the lawcourt, slave market and temple. Now picture Jesus in your place each time and pour out praises to him.*

Day 5

ROMANS 3:25B-26

Q: *What does the cross show (v 25, 26)?*

Q: *How does the cross show that God takes sin seriously—that is, that he is "just"?*

Q: *How does the cross show that sinners can be forgiven—that God is "the justifier"?*

If God did not judge sin, it would mean he was indifferent to suffering and injustice. God should and will judge us—the wonder is that he judges us in his Son. God bore God's judgment. He does not set his justice aside—he turns it onto himself. All the sins of his children—both those who lived before the cross and whose sins he had "passed over" (v 25), and those who would live after the cross—were justly judged and punished in the person of his Son. The cross is not a compromise between God's justice and God's love—it is the way that he satisfies both, fully. The cross is where God is seen to be just *and* the justifier; where we see the awesome beauty of both the righteousness *of* God and the righteousness *from* God.

Q: *What goes wrong in our lives if we see God as loving, but not just?*

Q: *What goes wrong if we see him as just, but not loving?*

Timothy Keller puts it like this: the cross shows us that God "is a Father worth having, and a Father we can have."

PRAY: *Praise God, your just justifier: and ask that you will live in a way that enjoys both his justice and his forgiveness.*

Day 6

Having shown us what we are redeemed from, and how we are redeemed, Paul begins to set out redemption's joys. The start of chapter 5 focuses on the believer; as we've seen, chapter 8 will widen the lens to the whole of creation.

ROMANS 5:1-6

Q: *If by faith we are now justified in God's sight, what do we know we have (v 1)?*

Paul is talking here about an objective reality, not a subjective feeling. It does not fluctuate based on feelings; peace has been declared by God. We are free from war with the divine.

Q: *What have we "obtained" (v 2)?*

A Christian is free to walk into the throneroom of the universe, right up to the throne, and say to the One who sustains each star and rules each atom: "Father..." You have access now through prayer; one day, you will stand there.

Q: *What do we now rejoice in (v 2b)? What part does suffering play in this (v 3-4)?*

Since our greatest joy is the prospect of seeing God in glory (v 2b), no trial can remove our joy, since it cannot remove our God. We are free from seeking joy in our circumstances or possessions or relationships; we are free to find it in the only place that will not fade or fail—God. Suffering enables the redeemed believer to appreciate redemption more deeply.

PRAY: *Reflect on why you need redemption, how you were given redemption, and what you enjoy through redemption. Pray that you would live out your redemption today—that it would affect all you think, all you feel and all you do.*

 **JOURNAL**

What I've learned or been particularly struck by this week...

What I want to change in my perspectives or actions as a result of this week...

Things I would like to think about more or discuss with others at my church...

BIBLE STUDY

Discuss

When you think about the work of God's Holy Spirit in people, what do you think of him doing?

👉 READ EXODUS 31:1-11

> *⁶ I have called by name Bezalel the son of Uri, son of Hur, of the tribe of Judah and I have filled him with the Spirit of God, with ability and intelligence, with knowledge and all craftsmanship ... that they may make all that I have commanded you; the tent of meeting, and the ark of the testimony, and the mercy seat that is on it...*

God speaks these words to Moses on the top of Mount Sinai, at the end of his instructions about how the Israelites are to build the "tent of meeting" (also called the "tabernacle")—the place where God will dwell among his people. The whole of chapters 25 – 30 have been taken up with detailed instructions given to Moses by the LORD as to how the tent of meeting is to be constructed.

1. Why is Bezalel so good at his job?

2. Why has God's Spirit given Bezalel, Oholiab and "all able men ability" (v 6-11)?

3. Look at the aspects of the tent of meeting that God picks out in verses 7-11. What craftsman's skills will be required in order to do all this?

4. The tent of meeting's design was intricate, inside and out. There was a reason for this. It was meant to point the Israelites somewhere else...

Complete the table:

TABERNACLE	EDEN
The materials used in the tent of meeting (25:3-7)	The materials found in Eden (Genesis 2:12)
The lampstand that gives light to the tent of meeting looks like a _____ (25:31-39); The ark of the covenant in the center of the tent of meeting is where God meets Moses to _____ _____ (25:22)	In the center of Eden, there are two _____ representing _____ and _____ (Genesis 2:9, 16-17)
The tabernacle instructions are structured around the phrase _____ _____ (25:1; 30:11, 17, 22, 34; 31:1, 12), occuring _____ times	The creation is structured around the phrase _____ (Gen 1:3, 6, 9, 14, 20, 24, 26), occuring _____ times

TABERNACLE	EDEN
The instructions for building the tabernacle culminate in instructions about _____ (31:12-17)	The account of creation ends with a description of _____ (Gen 2:1-3).
Who is in the tent of meeting? (25:8)	Who is in the Garden of Eden? (2:21-22; 3:8)

5. What is the tent of meeting meant to remind the Israelites of?

_____

_____

_____

6. What were Adam and Eve put in Eden to do (Genesis 1:28; 2:15, 18)?

_____

_____

_____

7. How are Bezalel and Oholiab engaged in the same kind of work?

_____

_____

_____

8. How can we be engaged in the same kind of work?

Apply

FOR YOURSELF: What abilities and passions has the Spirit given you that you use in the workplace? How can you be engaged in extending Eden, with God's help and in co-operation with others? How does this both excite you about your work, and challenge you in the way you view and go about your work?

FOR YOUR CHURCH: How often do you encourage each other (both during the service and in your conversations afterwards) to have this view of your Monday-Friday lives? How will you, as a group, proactively pursue the promotion of this kind of view of your vocations?

Pray

FOR YOUR GROUP: Thank God that he cares about, empowers, and uses your work when it is done under his rule, for his glory. Share how you find it hard to see your work in this way, and pray for one another.

FOR YOUR CHURCH: Pray that you would be a community that challenges one another to see work as a way to be part of God's purposes for his world; and a church that equips you for your weekly work, whether in the home, the field, the factory or the office, as well as for your Sunday worship.

SERMON NOTES

Bible passage: Date:

SESSION 4:

GLORIFYING GOD THROUGH WORK

HAVE YOU EVER SEEN YOUR WORKPLACE AS A GREAT
PLACE FOR YOUR OWN DISCIPLESHIP – A PLACE WHERE
YOU CAN REALLY GROW AND SERVE? IN THIS SESSION,
WE'LL CONNECT OUR COMMITMENT TO FOLLOWING CHRIST
WITH OUR LIVES FROM MONDAY TO FRIDAY.

GLORIFYING GOD THROUGH WORK

▶ **WATCH DVD 4.1 OR LISTEN TO TALK 4.1**

Discuss

How did you react to Tom's "confession" of having failed his church?

Which of these errors are you more likely to fall into?

- Thinking you can only please God through your work if it directly promotes the gospel.

73

- Thinking of yourself as a Christian only when involved in church activity.

▶ WATCH DVD 4.2 OR LISTEN TO TALK 4.2

Discuss

 **READ MATTHEW 11:28-30**

Jesus said:

28 Come to me, all who labor and are heavy laden, and I will give you rest. 29 Take my yoke upon you, and learn from me, for I am gentle and lowly in heart, and you will find rest for your souls. 30 For my yoke is easy, and my burden is light.

As you think of Jesus' image of a yoke, what do you find most encouraging? What is most challenging?

1. A YOKE FOR ALL OF LIFE

If Jesus' yoke is for all of life, that means **everything** we do, including our daily occupation, paid or otherwise. *"Jesus does not necessarily call us to change our job, but he does challenge us about how we do our job."* How have you been challenged so far while working through this curriculum?

2. A CUSTOM-MADE YOKE

"Your work situation is a custom-made yoke for you. Jesus is using the unique way you are wired and gifted, along with the work situation you find yourself in, to provoke and lead you to maturity." Think about the seven areas we looked at:

- To love your neighbor

- To love justice

- To share the gospel

- To do good work, well done

- To create beauty

- To worship God

- To enable generosity

Which of these primarily apply to how you serve God in your own work situation? How have you seen this play out in your work?

In the DVD presentation, Tom described the workplace as being like a classroom, where God is teaching us, and where we can learn and practice. In which of these areas do you feel you have the most need to learn and practice? What are some practical ways in which you can grow in these areas?

▶ WATCH DVD 4.3 OR LISTEN TO TALK 4.3

Discuss

3. A YOKE THAT OFFERS REST

Why is it liberating to tie our identity to Christ and not to our work?

If your work is frustrating, why is the "rest" of Jesus such good news?

If you love your job or are successful in your work, what does the "rest" of Jesus help you remember?

In both cases, what difference will this make in the coming week?

Pray

"Come to me, all who labor and are heavy laden, and I will give you rest. Take my yoke upon you, and learn from me, for I am gentle and lowly in heart, and you will find rest for your souls. For my yoke is easy, and my burden is light."

Pray through each line of Jesus' words in turn, thanking him for his promise of rest, and asking him to help you learn from him as you "take his yoke upon you."

DAILY BIBLE DEVOTIONALS

"For most of us, work is the place where we most regularly spend time with those who are not believers," said Tom. Colossians 4:2-6 helps equip us to witness at work.

Day 1

COLOSSIANS 4:2

Q: *What three hallmarks of prayer does Paul tell us to display?*

Q: *To what extent does your pattern of praying take account of each of these?*

But as we pray in a disciplined way, watching for our prayers being answered in, through and around us, and praising God for those answers, what are we to pray about? The context of this verse gives some content for the prayers. In the next verse, Paul will ask for prayer "that God may open to us a door for the word" (v 3). We are to pray about *witness*—ours, and our Christian friends'. In the previous section (3:22 – 4:1), Paul has been addressing bondservants and masters—that is, believers' conduct in a specific work context. We are to pray about our *work* relationships.

Many of us pray for many things. Some of us pray little for little things. Colossians 4:2 should serve to help us check: Do our prayers include prayers about our witness? Do they include requests about our work? And, putting the two together, are we speaking to our Lord about our witness at our work?

PRAY: *Pray for these things now—and pray for ongoing discipline, alertness and praise in your prayers.*

Day 2

COLOSSIANS 4:3

If even Paul needed the prayers of others, then we certainly do. Asking others to pray for us is a sign of wisdom, not of weakness.

Q: *What does Paul ask for prayer for?*

The "mystery" is "Christ in you, the hope of glory" (1:27). This is the gospel: the glorious King lives in us now, and we will live with the King in his glory in eternity.

Q: *When was the last time you asked God to "open a door" in your workplace for you to share the gospel?*

Q: *Where is Paul writing from (4:3)? Why is he there, does he suggest?*

Paul saw his prison as a mission field. He wanted an open door, not to walk into freedom but to talk about Jesus. Your workplace may be apathetic about or hostile to Christian faith—but have you considered that this may be the very reason God chose to put you in that place? Our circumstances must never be used as an excuse for not witnessing; rather, we need to learn to see our circumstances as an opportunity for witnessing.

PRAY: *Ask God to open a door for the gospel in your workplace, and give you the desire and ability to walk through it.*

Day 3

COLOSSIANS 4:4

Q: *How does Paul pray about how he declares the gospel? Given his calling and experience, why might it surprise us that he needs prayer for this?*

Clarity is a necessity in our witness. And we can be unclear in two ways. First, by non-declaration—by not speaking of a crucial part of the gospel message, which may avoid giving offense but also obscures the glory of Christ. Second, by over-complication—if we seek to give an exhaustive declaration, we give no clear explanation at all!

Clarity is a supernatural gift. It was for Paul, and so it is for us. We need to pray not only that we will share the gospel, but that we will share it well—that we will be clear and compelling, presenting the gospel in such a way that it touches the hopes and fears, and addresses the doubts and misunderstandings, of the person we are speaking to. God will help us do all that we "ought" to do.

Q: *Do non-believers you regularly work with know the content of the gospel? How might they hear it from you?*

Q: *Imagine you stepped into an elevator, and someone hit the button for the top floor, and then turned to you and said: "What is the message of Christianity?" Could you answer, clearly, in a minute?*

PRAY: *Pray for clarity. Pray for help to avoid non-declaration and over-complication. Pray that, in a year, your co-workers will have heard the gospel clearly from your lips.*

Day 4

COLOSSIANS 4:5

Q: *How do we need to live when we are with "outsiders"? What might this mean in your own day-to-day life?*

Q: *What is the link between walking in a godly way and speaking gospel truth?*

Time is short—we need to make best use of it. Jesus is returning, and we do not know his schedule—so we need to ensure we are doing all we can in the way we live to win opportunities to share Christ with "outsiders" in the way we speak. Everything we do today should be done in light of that coming day.

And this must impact the manner of our conduct as much as the content of our message. If we do not walk the gospel, we will not be able to talk the gospel. To "walk in wisdom" means that your reaction to stresses and strains, triumphs and failures at work will demonstrate that your hope lies in your future, not in your present. It means that Spirit-given wisdom and not worldly ambition, or office culture, or a desire for reputation are to direct the way we live. Whether our work is in the field, factory, office or home, wisdom should guide our steps.

Q: *Is your conduct undergirding or undermining your efforts to share the gospel (and the efforts of other Christians in your workplace)?*

PRAY: *Ask God to help you remember that time is short, and the way you live matters. Speak to him about any areas where you find it hard to know how to walk in wisdom.*

Day 5

COLOSSIANS 4:6

It is easy to live as though the only interactions we have that God cares about are "gospel conversations." But "ordinary" ones matter too. In fact, the second can lead, and should be leading, to the first.

Q: *"Grace" is a good one-word summary both of God's character and the gospel's content. So what is a "gracious" conversation (v 6a), do you think?*

Q: *Can you think of common topics of discussion in your workplace into which you could introduce an aspect of the gospel or your Christian life? How?*

Consider how salt changes the flavor of a meal. What we say, and the manner in which we say it, should have the same effect on the places where we live and work (v 6a). If you never mention the gospel, or your tone goes against the grain of the gospel, it is hardly surprising that people don't ask you about the gospel! Our everyday conversations should be salty, scattered with distinctive, attractive grains of gospel truth. These kinds of interactions, when accompanied by a wisdom-directed walk (v 5), are what open doors to us sharing the gospel.

So if you would like the door to open, and yet it never seems to, ask yourself: *Is what I say, and the way I say it, sufficiently salty?*

PRAY: *Ask God to help you with your everyday workplace conversations—to see how to sprinkle your interactions with something of the gospel in a natural way.*

Day 6

COLOSSIANS 4:6

If we do walk in wisdom... make the most of the time... and season our conversation with gracious salt...

Q: *What does the end of verse 6 imply people will then do?*

Q: *So what must we be ready to do?*

People do not always like the taste of salt. So sometimes, we will need to "know how ... to answer" these accusations—attacks on the way we choose to live, or what we declare we believe. But at other times, our gracious salt will lead people to be intrigued, and want to know what it is that we have and that they are missing. We will need to "know how ... to answer" these invitations. Each opportunity will require a different type of response.

Not only that, but "each person" will need to be spoken to differently. Everyone in your workplace comes with their own backstory, belief system, and set of burdens, dreams and disappointments. In order to know how to share the gospel well, we must first know people well.

Q: *Consider three or four people you work closely with. What are their burdens, dreams and disappointments? How might the gospel connect with these?*

Q: *Are you ready to answer well the most common accusations against Christianity you hear? How will you equip yourself?*

PRAY: *Re-read 4:2-6, and with your workplace in mind, pray about your witness.*

 **JOURNAL**

What I've learned or been particularly struck by this week...

What I want to change in my perspectives or actions as a result of this week...

Things I would like to think about more or discuss with others at my church...

BIBLE STUDY

Discuss

If you were to ask a random group of people in the street what they think of Christians and churches, what are some of the answers you think they might give? Do you think their assessment would be fair?

READ COLOSSIANS 3:1-17

> [7] In these you too once walked, when you were living in them. [8] But now you must put them all away: anger, wrath, malice, slander, and obscene talk from your mouth.

1. What has already happened to Christians, according to Paul in v 1-3? What do you think these statements mean?

What will happen in the future (v 4)?

2. What does Paul say should drive our thinking about life now?

3. Some people accuse Christians of being "so heavenly minded that they are of no earthly use." How would you reply to that accusation from this passage?

4. What does an understanding of our new life in Christ lead us to do (v 5)? Which of the qualities in verses 5 and 8 do you struggle most to leave behind, especially in the course of your daily occupation?

5. What further encouragements are there to work at growing in our holiness (v 6, 12)? How will we grow in our godliness (v 10, 16)?

6. How will the qualities of your renewed life (v 11-14) be distinctive in the place where you work?

7. How might your workplace be more enjoyable, and more productive and efficient, if it displayed the qualities in verses 12-13?

8. What does it mean to do "everything in the name of the Lord Jesus"? What will verse 17 mean in practice for you in the workplace?

Apply

FOR YOURSELF: What one quality can you work on growing in your life this week that will be especially beneficial to you and your colleagues at work?

FOR YOUR CHURCH: How can you encourage the peace of Christ to rule among you? How can you encourage the word of Christ to dwell more richly among you? What does "teaching and admonishing one another" look like in your congregational life? How can you encourage a communal sense of gratitude toward God to characterize your lives, rather than grumbling, discord and discontent?

Pray

FOR YOUR GROUP: Pray for your specific answers in question 4. Ask the Lord to help you recognize how and when you are tempted to live this way, and to bring to mind our privilege and status as chosen children. Spend some time giving thanks for your work—both the great things, and the things you find difficult and struggle with.

FOR YOUR CHURCH: Pray that the qualities of our renewed life would be evident in your whole church, and that you would each continue to grow as the word of Christ dwells richly among you.

SERMON NOTES

Bible passage: Date:

SESSION 5:

THE GOSPEL
AND YOUR WORK

ALL OF US HAVE A "STORY" THROUGH WHICH WE SEE THE
WORLD, OUR LIVES, AND OUR WORK. THAT STORY, FOR
EACH OF GOD'S PEOPLE, NEEDS TO BE THE GOSPEL. BUT
WHAT WILL THAT LOOK LIKE FOR OUR APPROACH TO OUR
OCCUPATION? HOW MIGHT THAT SHAPE OUR VIEW OF
OTHERS? AND WHAT CAN A RELATIONSHIP BETWEEN A
MASTER AND HIS SLAVE IN THE FIRST CENTURY TEACH US
ABOUT OUR LIVES IN THE TWENTY-FIRST?

THE GOSPEL AND YOUR WORK

▶ **WATCH DVD 5.1 OR LISTEN TO TALK 5.1**

Discuss

 **READ PHILEMON V 10-17**

¹⁰ *I appeal to you for my child, Onesimus, whose father I became in my imprisonment.* ¹¹ *(Formerly he was useless to you, but now he is indeed useful to you and to me.)* ¹² *I am sending him back to you, sending my very heart.* ¹³ *I would have been glad to keep him with me, in order that he might serve me on your behalf during my imprisonment for the gospel,* ¹⁴ *but I preferred to do nothing without your consent in order that your goodness might not be by compulsion but of your own accord.* ¹⁵ *For this perhaps is why he was parted from you for a while, that you might have him back forever,* ¹⁶ *no longer as a bondservant but more than a bondservant, as a beloved brother—especially to me, but how much more to you, both in the flesh and in the Lord.* ¹⁷ *So if you consider me your partner, receive him as you would receive me.*

93

How does Paul refer to the slave Onesimus? What does Paul think of him?

What appeal does Paul make to Philemon?

Why might Philemon find it difficult to accept Onesimus "as a beloved brother"?

▶ WATCH DVD 5.2 OR LISTEN TO TALK 5.2

Discuss

What stories does our culture tell us about being employed, and being an employer?

How does the gospel message challenge those stories, both for employer and employee?

Which story do you tell yourself most often during a working week? What effect does this have on you?

▶ WATCH DVD 5.3 OR LISTEN TO TALK 5.3

Discuss

What do you think is the difference between someone who calls themselves "a Christian plumber" and someone who would describe themselves as "a plumber who is also a Christian"?

Imagine holding up a sign like the ones at the start of the DVD. It says: "I am a
_____" (fill in your own daily occupation). Now put the word "Christian"
in front of your occupation. Is this how you usually see yourself? What difference
would it / does it make to how you view your daily occupation?

How do the people you work with see you? As a _____ who also
happens to be a Christian? Or do they see you as a Christian _____?
And if it's the first, what changes might you make so that they come to see you as
the second instead?

Pray

Has the letter to Philemon challenged the way in which you are viewing your own
daily occupation? Talk to God about your answers.

Thank God for the gospel story—creation, fall, redemption and new creation.
Thank him that you are part of that story because of Jesus.

Ask God to help you to view the whole of your life, including work, through the
gospel story.

DAILY BIBLE DEVOTIONALS

We have seen how the gospel story changes our view of our work relationships. This week, we focus on how Peter's first letter applies the gospel to our workplaces.

Day 1

1 PETER 2:11-12

Q: *How are Christians described (v 11)?*

Our stay here is temporary. We are visitors—"sojourners"—on the way home (read 1:3-4).

Q: *Why should we "keep [our] conduct among the Gentiles honorable" (v 12)?*

Q: *In what sense does this begin within us, rather than around us (v 11)?*

Because we know the gospel, we know how the story ends—with the return of the Lord Jesus in judgment and salvation. We want to live in such a way that unbelievers around us realize they are wrong to speak against his people, and so put their trust in him now and glorify him in joy, not terror, on that day.

We need to see our workplaces as mission fields, not as battlefields. In fact, the battle is within us—against "the passions of the flesh": our sinful desires, which would sell us a different story about how to find fulfillment and life, and would drag us from the gospel.

Q: *You are an exile, and your workplace is a mission field. Does your view of yourself and your work need to change?*

PRAY: *Pray that the end of the gospel story would shape the way you view work.*

Day 2

1 PETER 2:13-17

Q: *Who are we to be "subject" to (v 13-14)? Why is "every" (v 13) challenging?*

Q: *What motivation does Peter give for obeying the authorities over us (v 15)?*

Q: *Read Acts 5:17-18, 27-32. Are there limits to this obedience? What?*

We are "free" (1 Peter 2:16)—free from ruler-worship, where we either think they will fix everything, or worry that they will break everything. We know the One who placed them in power. We know that he rules supremely, and will return. But we are not free to sin, because we are free servants of God (v 16), and we serve him by obeying authorities. Not only that, we "honor" our rulers (v 17). Whether we voted for them or disagree with them, we speak of them respectfully, for it was God's choice to set them there.

This will impact our work practices. At work, Christians do not cut legal corners; or ignore unenforced laws; or speak ill of their rulers.

Q: *How does this need to shape your deeds and your words at work (and elsewhere)?*

PRAY: *Pray that you would be known as a law-abiding, authority-respecting person.*

Day 3

1 PETER 2:18-20

Peter is writing to first-century household slaves, some of whom may have held positions of responsibility, but who nevertheless were not free. With care, we can apply the principles Peter gives them to our modern working lives.

Q: *How should Christians treat their masters, or bosses? What difference does it make whether the boss is good or not (v 18)?*

Q: *How does Peter motivate his readers to live like this (v 19-20)?*

Notice that Peter uses the word "gracious" in both v 19 and 20. He is saying that God loves to reward faithfulness—to be generous to those who have borne unjust suffering because they lived in a way that was more "mindful of God" than their own advancement or reputation. Peter is echoing what Jesus had taught him: "Blessed are you when others revile you and persecute you … on my account … for your reward is great in heaven" (Matthew 5:11-12). There may be no reward for living as a Christian in your workplace—but there will be a heavenly reward from the Lord for living in a way that is mindful of him. So we "[endure] sorrows" without seeking to gain revenge, or compromise our conduct, or undermine our boss—however unfair they are being. For God sees that, and he is pleased by that.

Q: *Are you being called to endure sorrow while blessing your boss? How?*

PRAY: *Ask God to help you live more mindfully of his opinion than your own, or that of others.*

Day 4

Because Western culture has been broadly pro-Christian for the last few centuries, we tend to think deep down that there is a way to live that is both Christian and comfortable. But, says Peter, this is not our calling…

1 PETER 2:21

Q: *Whose steps are we called to follow, and what will this involve?*

Q: *Read Mark 8:34-38. In what sense is Peter simply summarizing Jesus' own teaching about following him?*

"Example" is a word that refers to children tracing out letters in order to learn how to write. We are to trace Jesus' steps. Our Master is our suffering Servant; and because he suffered for us, we are to expect to suffer like him. And as we do, we can remember where his steps lead; through suffering, to glory.

So unjust suffering, in the workplace and elsewhere, is not a sign that we've done something wrong. It is an indication that we're following the One who suffered for us. This will be of great hope to you if you know what it is to "keep your conduct among the Gentiles honorable" and have others "speak against you" (1 Peter 2:12). And this will be greatly challenging to you if your approach at work is to keep your head down, blend in and prioritize comfort over Christ.

Q: *So is this a word of hope or challenge to you? Why?*

PRAY: *Thank God for calling you to follow Jesus through suffering to glory. Pray you would trace his steps well.*

Day 5

1 PETER 2:22-23

Q: *In what four ways did Jesus NOT react when he faced unjust suffering?*

Q: *Why, when suffering unjustly at another's hands, is each of these reactions extremely tempting and even sensible-looking?*

Suffering tends to fire our instinct for self-preservation and self-vindication. That's why we use suffering as an excuse to sin, if sinning would stop it; as a reason to be economical with the truth, if lying would provide an escape route; as a justification to bite back or gain revenge, if reviling and threatening would make us feel better or look better. Yet as he stood on trial for his life, unjustly accused, deserted by his friends, spat at, punched, and whipped, Jesus did *none* of these. Pause to worship his perfection.

How did he do it? By "entrusting himself to him who judges justly" (v 23). He knew how the story ended—not with his death, but with his Father's justice. He cared more about the approval of his Father than the vindication of the world. He knew his Father would bring justice, so he did not need to take revenge. This is how he lived as he did—and how you can live as he did too.

Q: *In your work life, how and why do you sometimes react to others in one of those four ways? How would remembering v 23b help you respond in a way that follows Jesus' "example" (v 21)?*

PRAY: *Pray for specific situations, for grace to follow Jesus' steps.*

Day 6

1 PETER 2:24-25

In his trials and death, Jesus is our example; but he is also far more than our example.

Q: *In his time of greatest suffering, what caused his most acute suffering (v 24a)?*

Q: *What did he achieve (v 24)? Why was it necessary (v 25)?*

Why did Jesus bear our sins, paying the penalty for them? So that we might die daily to them, and "live to righteousness." His death transforms *what* we live for, *who* we live for, and who we live *like*—the Lord, not the world. His death has brought us into a new story with a different ending—the story Philemon and Onesimus had entered into, and which Paul showed must rework their view of their working relationships.

So reflect on your workplace, be it in an office, a factory, a field, your home, or elsewhere:

Q: *Do you see yourself as a visitor—a sojourner—not there to find ultimate fulfillment in your work but rather, to point to Christ in your conduct?*

Q: *Are you living subject to both the government and to your boss, even when that is hard or involves unjust treatment?*

Q: *Are you living mindful of God's approval... trusting in God's judgment... and grateful for Christ's suffering for you?*

PRAY: *Thank God for Jesus' death. Pray for grace joyfully to follow in his steps. Speak to God about specific situations you are struggling in, and particular aspects of your character you need him to change.*

JOURNAL

What I've learned or been particularly struck by this week…

What I want to change in my perspectives or actions as a result of this week…

Things I would like to think about more or discuss with others at my church…

BIBLE STUDY

Discuss

What different motivations do people have to work? Can you think of examples of people you know who are driven by each of these? What motivations have you had in some of the work you have done in the past?

In this Bible study, we are going to look at Paul's instructions to slaves and masters in the letter to the Colossians—sent at the same time as the letter to Philemon. Are you prepared to be challenged about your own attitude toward work?

👉 READ COLOSSIANS 3:22 – 4:6

> 23 *Whatever you do, work heartily, as for the Lord and not for men,* 24*knowing that from the Lord you will receive the inheritance as your reward. You are serving the Lord Christ.*

1. What qualities should bondservants or slaves bring to their obedience to earthly masters?

2. Why might these commands still be relevant, but hard to follow in your working situation?

3. What should motivate Christians to be different??

4. What help is there here for a slave who is working for a bad master? How will this help you when you are treated unfairly at work?

5. What qualities are Christian masters called to bring to their management of workers? Why?

6. Most of us are a long way from the world of bondservants, slaves and masters. How might there be different aspects to our obedience to these commands today?

7. How might 4:5-6 help us in the way we relate to non-Christian colleagues and managers?

Apply

FOR YOURSELF: Make a list of what your real motivations are for work. Try to be brutally honest about all the things that motivate you. If you are able to rank them, all the better.

FOR YOUR CHURCH: Where do the motivations we have discovered in today's Bible study fit in? In what practical ways can we encourage ourselves and each other to bring them higher up the list?

Pray

FOR YOURSELF: Pray that God would give you the right attitude as a worker or as a manager. Ask the Lord to help you be respectful, hard-working and focused on serving him in your daily occupation. Ask for opportunities to share the gospel at work.

FOR YOUR CHURCH: Pray that you would encourage one another to live the new life that the gospel brings—especially in your attitudes toward work. Pray that there would be a loving spirit of mutual encouragement.

SERMON NOTES

Bible passage: Date:

SESSION 6:

WORK AND POWER

ALL OF US HAVE SOME POWER AS WE DO OUR WORK.
WE ALL SHAPE OTHERS, AND OUR SURROUNDINGS,
FOR BETTER AND FOR WORSE. IN THIS SESSION,
YOU'LL BE INSPIRED AND CHALLENGED TO BRING
CHRISTIAN JOY AND HOPE TO THE PLACES WE GO
AND THE WAYS IN WHICH WE WORK.

WORK AND POWER

▶ WATCH DVD 6.1 OR LISTEN TO TALK 6.1

Discuss

☞ READ JEREMIAH 29:4-14

> ⁴ Thus says the Lord of hosts, the God of Israel, to all the exiles whom I have sent into exile from Jerusalem to Babylon: ⁵ Build houses and live in them; plant gardens and eat their produce. ⁶ Take wives and have sons and daughters; take wives for your sons, and give your daughters in marriage, that they may bear sons and daughters; multiply there, and do not decrease. ⁷ But seek the welfare of the city where I have sent you into exile, and pray to the Lord on its behalf, for in its welfare you will find your welfare. ⁸ For thus says the Lord of hosts, the God of Israel: Do not let your prophets and your diviners who are among you deceive you, and do not listen to the dreams that they dream, ⁹ for it is a lie that they are prophesying to you in my name; I did not send them, declares the Lord.

¹⁰ For thus says the Lord: When seventy years are completed for Babylon, I will visit you, and I will fulfill to you my promise and bring you back to this place. ¹¹ For I know the plans I have for you, declares the Lord, plans for welfare and not for evil, to give you a future and a hope. ¹² Then you will call upon me and come and pray to me, and I will hear you. ¹³ You will seek me and find me, when you seek me with all your heart. ¹⁴ I will be found by you, declares the Lord, and I will restore your fortunes and gather you from all the nations and all the places where I have driven you, declares the Lord, and I will bring you back to the place from which I sent you into exile.

What surprises you about what God says to these exiles? What might you have expected him to say?

What do you think it means to "seek the welfare" of a city (v 7)?

Why do you think God wants Israel to seek the welfare of Babylon?

▶ WATCH DVD 6.2 OR LISTEN TO TALK 6.2

Discuss

In what ways do you think you might have influence in your workplace? How might you use that influence to seek the common good with your work, and in your workplace?

👉 READ 1 THESSALONIANS 5:15

[15] See that no one repays anyone evil for evil, but always seek to do good to one another and to everyone.

What do you think seeking the common good should look like in your local community?

What is your workplace currently doing that contributes to the common good? What else could your workplace be doing?

▶ WATCH DVD 6.3 OR LISTEN TO TALK 6.3

Discuss

In the last few sessions we have been thinking about ways in which we can glorify God or serve God in our work; in other words, how we can "bloom where we are planted." Have you defined what some of these ways are for you personally? How have you been reminding yourself about them as you have gone about your work in the past couple of weeks?

Three possible ways of using your influence wisely are to 1) donate your skills, 2) invent, or 3) invest. Choose one of these and think about how you might do this in your own workplace.

Now think about how your church family can together seek the common good of your local community. Is there an issue that you could donate your combined skills to, invent a solution to between you, or invest in together? How might you start to do this?

Pray

"In the same way, let your light shine before others, so that they may see your good works and give glory to your Father who is in heaven."

Think about any non-Christians who see you in your daily workplace. Ask God to help you to live for him in such a way that "your light shines" before them, and they praise God as a result.

"For I know the plans I have for you, declares the Lord, plans for welfare and not for evil, to give you a future and a hope. Then you will call upon me and come and pray to me, and I will hear you. You will seek me and find me, when you seek me with all your heart."

Use these verses as the basis on which to pray for yourself, your workplace and your church.

DAILY BIBLE DEVOTIONALS

Like Jeremiah, the book of Daniel teaches us how to work well and worship God "in exile"—in a world made by him, that lives in rejection of him, but is yet loved by him.

Day 1

DANIEL 1:1-21

Verses 1-7 describe a disaster—the fall of Jerusalem, the capital's of God's land; the end of temple worship; and the removal of the movers and shakers to exile in Babylon.

Q: *What is the plan for these men (v 3-5)?*

This is not just about changing jobs, but about changing the exiles' identity (hence the name changes, v 6-7). Daniel and his friends are to be "Babylonized."

Q: *What did they refuse to do (v 8)?*

Q: *What was the outcome, and why (v 11-20—see especially v 17)?*

"Daniel was there until the first year of King Cyrus" (v 21)—for many decades he used his God-given skill and wisdom to serve a pagan king. The easier options would have been to refuse to serve the king, or to become fully Babylonized and reject God; instead he took the harder, godly option—working hard for Babylon, but not compromising his obedience to God.

Q: *What does it look like for you to take this harder option in your work?*

PRAY: *Ask God for the help you need to live under his rule, working hard for others.*

Day 2

DANIEL 2:1-49

The king's troubling dreams cost him sleep (v 1); but by verse 6, they threaten to cost his advisers their lives. By v 13, the wise men are "about to be killed"—working for the king did not offer much job (or life) security. And Daniel and his friends are on the hitlist…

Q: *How does Daniel respond to the king and to his friends (v 16-18)?*

Time and time again, we see these exiled men leaving the outcome to God, and focusing on being godly in their conduct. So here, they lean not on their own wisdom but beg God to have mercy and give them his. And when God answers prayer, Daniel pauses to praise him (v 19-23).

Q: *Is this your response to a work problem, small or great? Prayer… and then praise? If not, why not, and how will you change?*

Q: *How does Daniel use his growing influence to protect others (v 24)? Witness to others (v 26-28)? Seek good for others (v 48-49)?*

Q: *How can you use your work position to do these three things?*

PRAY: *Use your answers to the final question to shape your prayers today.*

Day 3

DANIEL 3:1-30

Q: *What choice confronts Daniel's friends by verse 15?*

When something we hold dear is threatened, we discover whether we hold it as more precious than we do God. In Western work, it is unlikely to be our life; but how easily we excuse compromising our obedience to God when our position, bonus or promotion are at risk. However hard and honestly we work (as these men did), there will be times when we must choose.

Q: *What do the three men know God can do? Do they know he will do it (v 16-18)?*

God does not promise always to give us what we think we need. He *can* rescue us from any adverse outcomes that result from living for him; but we do not know that he *will*. What we do know, as these three men discovered, is that he will be with us in the furnace (v 25). And what we also know is that God will bring us through the final furnace, the fire of his judgment. Since we need not fear the ultimate outcome, we need fear no adverse outcome in this life. We, like these men, are free to obey God, even when we stand alone and even when we must lose out. Daniel 3 shows we have no excuse for compromise; but also that we don't need to find one.

Q: *In your work life, how are you influenced or told to worship and obey something other than God? How could you live like these men in those moments?*

PRAY: *Ask that God would be more precious than your work, so that you risk obeying him.*

Day 4

By Daniel 5, a new king, Belshazzar, is on the throne. And the focus is on Daniel, now an old man, still working for the king of Babylon.

DANIEL 5:1-30

His predecessor had come to recognize Daniel's God (4:34-37); but Belshazzar actively mocks him, using the temple vessels to get drunk and worship other gods (5:2-4). This is not an easy man to desire to serve. But when the king needs the writing on the wall (v 5) to be interpreted, Daniel is sent for (v 13).

Q: *What does the king offer Daniel, and how does Daniel respond (v 16-17)?*

Q: *What does Daniel know, which means the king's offer in v 16 is empty (v 23-28)?*

Q: *Given the sort of king this was, and given what Daniel knows will happen, why might it have been tempting for Daniel not to tell the truth about the message?*

In a sense, all believers stand where Daniel did. We experience the offers of glittering trinkets in this world; we know the ultimate end of all who reject God in this world. All that glitters is not godly, and what is godly often does not sparkle. But when we serve a greater, eternal King, we are able to risk speaking the truth, and to reject the offers of the world even when they almost dazzle us.

Q: *Are you at risk at work of chasing worldly trinkets, or of failing to speak the truth to protect yourself? What needs to change?*

PRAY: *Pray that an eternal perspective will affect everything you do and say.*

Day 5

DANIEL 5:31 – 6:28

Q: *What similarities are there between this episode and the one experienced by Daniel's friends in chapter 3? Do you see any significant differences?*

Q: *Why do you think Daniel didn't begin to shut the windows and close the curtains when he prayed (6:10)?*

Often, it is not sins of commission (things we should not do, but do anyway) that are our greatest problem, but sins of omission (things we should do, but do not). Daniel could have saved himself by omitting to pray, or even by praying where he could not be seen. But he would not. Instead, he lived out a public faith, which he refused to push to the margins or banish to the realm of his private life.

Our faith is to be proclaimed not only in safe places—at church on a Sunday, at home with the family—but also in the riskier sphere of public work, day by day. A wholly private faith is not an obedient faith. Again, we are being asked the question: *What do we value more: serving God or serving our safety?*

Q: *How does this encourage and/or challenge you specifically in your work life?*

Q: *How does the king end up responding in v 25-28? How does this motivate you to live with public, uncompromising faith?*

PRAY: *Thank God that he uses risk-taking, public faith to change people—and ask him to enable you to live in this way.*

Day 6

How could Daniel live in this way, year after year? And how can we really live this way too? Daniel 7 gives us the answer: *We will live for God as he did if we know God as he did.*

DANIEL 7:1-14

Daniel saw this vision *before* he stood before Belshazzar or faced the lion's den (v 1).

Q: *What impression do verses 2-8 give us of worldly kingdoms (the beasts)? How does this make v 9-12 awe-inspiring?*

Q: *Who approaches the Ancient of Days— God—and what is he given (v 13-14)?*

Q: *How would this vision have equipped Daniel to live as he did, do you think?*

As he labored for the most powerful empire in his world, Daniel knew who truly ruled (v 9). As he faced the might of pagan kings, Daniel knew who would ultimately win (v 10-12). As he considered the end of his earthly life, Daniel knew what would last (v 14). *And you know all this too.* Not only that—we have seen in glorious high definition what he only glimpsed in shadow. We know that "the Son of Man came" to live on earth, and we know the astounding truth that he used his power "not to be served, but to serve, and to give his life as a ransom for many" (Mark 10:45). You know the Son of Man. You know Jesus. And you can, and must, live for God as Daniel did, because you know God as he did.

PRAY: *Ask God to enable you to know, in your heart as well as your head, what Daniel knew—and to live in light of that every day.*

121

JOURNAL

What I've learned or been particularly struck by this week…

What I want to change in my perspectives or actions as a result of this week…

Things I would like to think about more or discuss with others at my church…

BIBLE STUDY

Discuss

Have you ever met someone who is really "important"—either because of their position, or something they achieved? What did it feel like for you to meet them? How did they behave? How do you feel about them now?

READ MARK 10:32-45

Jesus said:

44 *"Whoever would be great among you must be your servant, and whoever would be first among you must be slave of all. 45 For even the Son of Man came not to be served but to serve, and to give his life as a ransom for many.*

An extraordinary scene unfolds: Jesus is striding along the road to Jerusalem with purpose and resolution; the disciples are following behind, some amazed, more of them terrified about what is about to happen. Then he turns to explain to them what is going on…

1. What does Jesus tell his disciples? Why is it so amazing that Jesus tells them this at this particular moment? (Hint: Think about what he is doing as he speaks, v 22.)

2. What are James and John asking for in verse 37? What do you think about the way that they make their request?

3. What is the meaning of the questions that Jesus asks them in verse 36? What does their answer to him reveal about their understanding of his mission, and the statement he made in verses 33-34?

4. What does Jesus promise them life will be like in his service (v 39-40)? Why are we so attracted to versions of Christianity which seem to promise us comfort, ease and success?

5. What is the fundamental attitude toward power that Jesus wants his followers to embody? How is this different from the way power is used in the world (see verses 42-45)?

6. How should this principle be worked out in church structures and relationships? How far is it legitimate to take this principle for Christian living into our daily work? Are there any limitations on how this should be applied to our work in the world?

Apply

FOR YOURSELF: What power do you have—at home, in church and at work? How do you wield it—as a Christ-like servant, or as a self-centered leader? Can you think of one thing you can do that will help you serve in a more Christ-like way this week?

FOR YOUR CHURCH: Does your church have a culture of honesty, where people can share how they are struggling—or is there a general feeling that everyone is coping and doing well? How might you be part of the way in which your church becomes a more nurturing place for people who may be suffering in silence at the moment?

Pray

FOR YOU AND YOUR GROUP: Spend some time praising your Savior for his perseverance in the face of ultimate suffering. Thank the Lord that he became a servant so that we could be ransomed from slavery to sin and death. Pray that you would increasingly grow like him in humble service of one another.

FOR YOUR WORK: Pray for your individual working situations, and for the power that you have over others. Ask God for wisdom in how you express and use your power with others.

FOR THE CHURCH THROUGHOUT THE WORLD: Pray for your brothers and sisters worldwide who are facing hostile opposition every day—experiencing the "cup" and "baptism" of the Lord Jesus. Pray that those who are persecuted would continue to trust Jesus; that they would look to him, and persevere to his praise and glory. And pray that your own church, and particularly your leadership, would be models of humble service.

SERMON NOTES

Bible passage: Date:

SESSION 7:

WORK AND THE COMMON GOOD

THIS SESSION IS ABOUT ECONOMICS — BUT NOT ONLY
NATIONAL-LEVEL QUESTIONS OF TAXATION AND
SPENDING, BUT ALSO DAY-TO-DAY, INDIVIDUAL DECISIONS
ABOUT HOW WE USE WHAT WE HAVE BEEN GIVEN. WE'LL
LEARN TO THINK DIFFERENTLY ABOUT THE CHOICES WE
MAKE EVERY DAY, AND HOW THEY CAN BE SHAPED BY
THE GOSPEL FOR THE GOOD OF THOSE AROUND US.

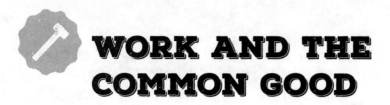

WORK AND THE COMMON GOOD

▶ **WATCH DVD 7.1 OR LISTEN TO TALK 7.1**

Discuss

 **READ MATTHEW 25:14-30**

¹⁶ *For [the kingdom of heaven] will be like a man going on a journey, who called his servants and entrusted to them his property …*

¹⁹ *After a long time the master of those servants came and settled accounts with them.* ²⁰ *And he who had received the five talents came forwards, bringing five talents more, saying, "Master, you delivered to me five talents; here I have made five talents more."* ²¹ *His master said to him, "Well done, good and faithful servant. You have been faithful over a little; I will set you over much. Enter into the joy of your master."*

The man going on a journey is a picture of the Lord Jesus, who left this world when he ascended to heaven, and will one day return to it in power and glory.

What should we be doing in the meantime, and how do the master's words in verses 21 and 23 motivate us to do this?

How does the third servant's description of the master's character in verses 24-25 show that he misunderstood what his master was like? Was he really a servant at all?

You are in charge of an economy that has been entrusted to you by Christ—your own! What is exciting about this idea?

▶ **WATCH DVD 7.2 OR LISTEN TO TALK 7.2**

Discuss

How can we, like the lawyer Jesus met, seek to limit the range of those whom we have to love? Why is this tempting?

What will go wrong with our day-to-day choices and bigger life choices when we forget to consider either:

- how to live with Christ-like compassion, or

- that we need to live within our economic capacity.

WATCH DVD 7.3 OR LISTEN TO TALK 7.3

Discuss

Which of the seven biblical economic principles that Tom listed did you find most surprising? interesting? challenging?

1. The value of private property

2. Safety from abuse of power

3. Dependable currency

4. Profit and incentive

5. Value added

6. Healthy families

7. Care for the poor

If there is no single, one-size-fits-all biblical economics, how should that affect the way we view politics, and the way we treat those with whom we disagree on economic or political issues?

As thoughtful students of the Bible we see that economics is first and foremost about creating blessing from the created order. Tom summarized economics as being "how we choose to use scarce resources that have alternative uses." Tom summarized economics as being *"how we choose to use scarce resources that have alternative uses."*
What economic decisions will you face this week?
How has this session empowered and challenged you about those economic choices?

Pray

"Well done, good and faithful servant. You have been faithful over a little; I will set you over much. Enter into the joy of your master."

Thank the Lord for the joy that lies before his people. Thank him for the prospect of hearing these words said in welcome to each of you.

Thank him for the particular time, energy, abilities and circumstances he has given you, and pray for yourself and the others in your group for the compassion and wisdom to know how best to serve him in how you use those gifts.

Thank God for those in your church who exemplify God-directed, God-glorifying daily choices with their "talents."

DAILY BIBLE DEVOTIONALS

Most of us work for money. And our salary is often the cause of concern, joy, hope, bitterness or pride. These devotionals will connect your paycheck to your gospel faith.

Day 1

LUKE 19:1-4

Q: *How is Zacchaeus described (v 2-3)?*

We all chase something that promises to satisfy us, give us security, and make us feel significant. For Zacchaeus, the "something" was money. Profit was the only motive for being a tax collector—Jews working for Rome were seen as traitors, trading reputation for money. To get rich as a tax collector meant charging extra and keeping the difference yourself, trading morality for money. Zacchaeus had traded both. He had given much for money, and he had made much money…

Q: *So why is it strange that he was so keen to catch a glimpse of a preacher who lived in poverty (v 4)?*

Money promises much, but ultimately fails us. It cannot buy what we most need in life; it cannot buy our way out of death. Zacchaeus had given much for money, and money had not given him much back, so he climbed that tree. Money whispers that it will solve all your problems and supply all your longing, and how easy it is to listen. But it is a lie.

Q: *How does money whisper to you?*

PRAY: *Ask God to help you see whether and where you could fall for money's lies.*

Day 2

LUKE 19:4-6

Q: *What did Jesus do once he had come to where Zacchaeus was (v 5)?*

Every other worldview, whether religious or secular, says: *You need to chase what you need to have.* Zacchaeus had chased money. Others chase experience, or promotion, or acceptance from a deity. Christianity says: *What you need to have has come to you.*

All Zacchaeus does is climb a tree—and Jesus tells him to get down. The rest is all about Jesus. Jesus moves to where Zacchaeus is. He looks up at him. He starts the conversation. He invites himself into Zacchaeus' house.

Q: *How did Zacchaeus react, in action and in emotion (v 6)?*

If Jesus has met with us and invited himself into our lives, this is how we feel too. As Zacchaeus came down the tree, only one thing in his life had changed; but Jesus had arrived, so everything had changed.

Q: *The source of our greatest joy indicates the source of our worship. What gives you most joy, and does anything take it?*

PRAY: *Pray that you would know the joy of truly knowing Jesus as the generous Giver of your satisfaction, security and significance.*

Day 3

LUKE 19:7-8

Q: How does meeting Jesus change Zacchaeus' actions with his money (v 8)?

Q: What do these actions suggest has changed in his attitude to his money?

The money that had been gathered so greedily is now given away generously. Zacchaeus is repenting; turning away from what he had worshiped because he now worships Jesus. He gives away what he had grasped for.

And in a materialist, consumerist society, where money whispers its lies to us each day, we will likely need to repent each day of worshiping money; of finding our joy in the money we have, or might have; of feeling good because we have more (or less) than others.

Q: When it comes to money, are there attitudes and/or actions you need to repent of?

Learn to repent as Zacchaeus did. Repentance does not always mean seeing what we worship as bad (he did not give all his money away); it does mean stopping seeing it as god. It does not mean doing the right thing to earn Jesus' friendship; it means doing the loving thing because of Jesus' friendship. So the power to repent comes not from disliking the false god, so much as loving the real one. As we look at Jesus, and find satisfaction, security and significance from him and in him, we find ourselves able joyfully to give away what we once thought we must have.

PRAY: Spend time looking at Jesus; and then spend time in repentance.

Day 4

LUKE 19:7, 9-10

Q: Remember who Zacchaeus was (v 2). In what sense was grumbling (v 7) at Jesus' actions toward him justified?

If we miss the offense of what Jesus is doing here, we miss the awesomeness of the gospel itself. Zacchaeus has ignored God, disowned his people, and trampled on those around him, all in worship of money. He is a traitor; a selfish, exploitative thief. Yet Jesus treats him as though he's done nothing wrong. How can this be just, fair or right?

Q: Read 18:31-33. Where was Jesus going as he passed through Jericho and met Zacchaeus? What would happen there?

Jesus had not just come to "seek … the lost," as he had sought Zacchaeus up his tree in Jericho. He had also come to "save the lost" (19:10), which he would achieve by climbing his own tree in Jerusalem—not a living, sycamore-fig tree, but a cross, a place of death. On his tree, Jesus would bear the punishment Zacchaeus deserved. On that tree, Zacchaeus would be judged, and so Zacchaeus could be called down from his tree into relationship with Jesus—into real, eternal life. Zacchaeus in his tree heard divine words of welcome because the Son of Man would hear divine words of condemnation on his.

And on the tree of death, Jesus would take your judgment and die your death too. Why would we worship money, or any other god, when the true God loves like this?

PRAY: Use v 10 to thank and praise your Savior.

Day 5

We turn from Zacchaeus' life to Paul's words.

1 TIMOTHY 6:6-10

Q: *What does true godliness bring (v 6)?*

Godliness is not a means to an end (v 5b); it is an end in itself. When we pursue Christ-likeness simply because we long to be like Christ, we find ourselves to be content.

Q: *How does verse 7 enable us to keep wealth and possessions in perspective?*

Q: *What is the danger of forgetting this and desiring the riches of this world (v 9-10)?*

There are material necessities we need in order to be content (v 8). But it is so very easy to forget (or refuse) to distinguish between needs and wants, necessities and luxuries. This forgetting or refusing is a sign that we do not truly believe Paul when he says that the desire to be rich, whatever end of the wealth spectrum we are on, has the potential to lead us to wander away from the faith (v 9-10). Pursuit of riches in this life tends to leads us to lose the riches of the next life—because, as the Lord himself said: "Where your treasure is, there your heart will be also … You cannot serve both God and money" (Matt. 6:21, 24).

Q: *Do you believe the words of Paul and Jesus here? What difference will they make to your view of the financial aspects of your work such as salary, pay rises, job moves or bonuses?*

PRAY: *Thank God for all he has provided for you. Pray your contentment will spring from the God you know, not the wealth you have.*

Day 6

It is not unholy to be wealthy; it is what you do with your wealth that counts.

1 TIMOTHY 6:11-19

Q: *What two mistakes do the wealthy need to be reminded to avoid (v 17)?*

Q: *What are the wealthy to do with their wealth (v 18)?*

The danger of wealth is that we place our hope in the riches, rather than the Giver of those riches (v 17). The opportunity of wealth is that we can serve that Giver with those riches (v 18).

Q: *What does this allow wealthy believers to do (v 19)?*

This true life is what Paul calls "eternal life" back in v 12, where Timothy is also called to "take hold" of it. Eternal life isn't only about quantity; it is also about quality. It has begun now, and is every Christian's now; but it needs to be embraced and enjoyed by us now so that we may experience "the life that is truly life" (v 19, NIV2011). Quality of life is not secured by greater wealth, but by greater appreciation of all that we already have in Christ, and all that we will one day enjoy with Christ (v 14-16).

Q: *Consider both Zacchaeus' example and Paul's teachings. How is wealth (either what you have or what you would like to have) a danger to you in your faith and godliness? How is what you do have an opportunity for you to live out your faith and grow in godliness?*

PRAY: *Read Proverbs 30:8-9 and make that the basis for your prayers today.*

 **JOURNAL**

What I've learned or been particularly struck by this week...

What I want to change in my perspectives or actions as a result of this week...

Things I would like to think about more or discuss with others at my church...

BIBLE STUDY

Discuss

If someone looked at your daily or weekly calendar, or the things you thought important to list in your diary, what might they conclude about what is really important to you?

👉 READ JAMES 4:13 – 5:6

> *17Whoever knows the right thing to do and fails to do it, for him it is sin."*

James is writing a book of "gospel-shaped wisdom" for Christians living in the real world. In this passage he focuses our attention on the choices we make in using two scarce resources: time and money!

1. Who is James speaking to in these verses (4:13)? What does their priority appear to be?

2. What perspectives does James say gospel-shaped people should have, which will drive them to make different choices (v 14, 15)?

3. How does verse 15 help us to see why the attitude of verse 13 is, as James puts it, "arrogant", "boasting" and "evil" (v 16)?

4. Why is it good news that God is in charge of the future? How should these verses affect both how we plan, and what we plan?

5. Who is James speaking to in 5:1-6? And what does he warn them about?

6. How might we end up living like the people James takes aim at here?

7. What has James taught us about what "godly" economics is? What aspect did you find most challenging or thought-provoking?

Apply

FOR YOURSELF: It is very easy for us to make plans or use our money without reference to God's priorities for life and his loving control over all things. How can you be more prayerful and godly in your planning and spending? When do you most need to remember consciously to bring these perspectives to mind?

FOR YOUR CHURCH: How can you cultivate conversations about these subjects that will encourage others to be godly in their decision-making? We are often very private about our spending choices, but also fearful that others will judge us for extravagance. How easy would you find it to rebuke or admonish a brother or sister for something they chose to spend their time and money on that might be unwise or unhelpful?

Pray

FOR YOUR GROUP: Ask the Lord to help you be honest about your own weaknesses and failures with each other, and that you would deal with each other gently and lovingly. Pray that you would be able to encourage each other to make good choices in the use of your time and money.

FOR YOUR CHURCH: Pray that your leaders would help church members grow in godliness and in the way you use your time and money. Pray for a growing sense that our loving Lord is sovereign over all things.

SERMON NOTES

Bible passage: Date:

SESSION 8:

WHAT WE ARE WORKING TOWARD

IN OUR FIRST SESSION WE LOOKED BACK AT THE CREATION OF THE WORLD. IN THIS LAST SESSION, WE LOOK FORWARD TO THE RE-CREATION OF THE WORLD — AND AS WE DO SO, WE'LL FIND MUCH MOTIVATION TO WORK HARD, WELL AND JOYFULLY IN OUR CURRENT SITUATION.

WHAT WE ARE WORKING TOWARD

Discuss

What are the primary images our culture uses to think about heaven?

When you think about eternity, what pictures come to your mind? Which do you find the most appealing or attractive?

 **WATCH DVD 8.1 OR LISTEN TO TALK 8.1**

Discuss

"In the new creation, we will work." How do you react to this statement?

 READ REVELATION 21:1-5 AND 22:1-5

¹ Then I saw a new heaven and a new earth, for the first heaven and the first earth had passed away, and the sea was no more. ² And I saw the holy city, new Jerusalem, coming down out of heaven from God, prepared as a bride adorned for her husband. ... **22** ³ No longer will there be anything accursed, but the throne of God and of the Lamb will be in it, and his servants will worship him. ... ⁵ And night will be no more. They will need no light of lamp or sun, for the Lord God will be their light, and they will reign forever and ever.

What kind of work do these verses describe: done by God? done by us?

 WATCH DVD 8.2 OR LISTEN TO TALK 8.2

Discuss

 READ ISAIAH 65:17, 21-25

> ¹⁷ "For behold, I create new heavens
>   and a new earth,
> and the former things shall not be remembered
>   or come into mind …
> ²¹ They shall build houses and inhabit them;
>   they shall plant vineyards and eat their fruit.
> ²² They shall not build and another inhabit;
>   they shall not plant and another eat;
> for like the days of a tree shall the days of my people be,
>   and my chosen shall long enjoy the work of their hands.
> ²³ They shall not labor in vain
>   or bear children for calamity,
> for they shall be the offspring of the blessed of the Lord,
>   and their descendants with them.
> ²⁴ Before they call I will answer;
>   while they are yet speaking I will hear.
> ²⁵ The wolf and the lamb shall graze together;
>   the lion shall eat straw like the ox,
>   and dust shall be the serpent's food.
> They shall not hurt or destroy
>   in all my holy mountain,"
> says the LORD.

Isaiah 65 is the other key passage, alongside Revelation 21 and 22, that describes the new creation. What does Isaiah 65 tell us about work in the new creation?

The following table sums up what we have learned about work during this curriculum. Use the Bible passages to fill in the blanks.

CREATION	THE FALL	REDEMPTION	NEW CREATION
Genesis 2:15	Genesis 3:16-19	Romans 8:19-23	Isaiah 65:21-23
God created us to _____	Work was _____ by the fall	Work is being renewed and transformed by _____	Work will _____ and _____ in the new creation

WATCH DVD 8.3 OR LISTEN TO TALK 8.3

WHAT WE ARE WORKING TOWARD

Discuss

In the DVD presentation, Tom says: *"We began in a garden, full of potential, called to work—and we will end in a city, full of potential, healed from the curse of the fall, and called to work as servants of the living God, and rulers with Christ in the new creation."*

How does the role of people in the Garden of Eden compare to our future role in the new creation?

How does knowing what we are looking forward to in the new creation help you when facing struggles with work today?

Look back over your notes and journal entries from the previous sessions.

- What have you been encouraged by?

- What have you been particularly challenged by?

● What changes have you made as a result?

Pray

"Then I saw a new heaven and a new earth, for the first heaven and the first earth had passed away, and the sea was no more. And I saw the holy city, new Jerusalem, coming down out of heaven from God, prepared as a bride adorned for her husband. And I heard a loud voice from the throne saying, "Behold, the dwelling place of God is with man. He will dwell with them, and they will be his people, and God himself will be with them as their God."

Ask God to help you serve him faithfully as you look forward to being with him in the new creation.

Look at some of the practical things you have written on this page. Pray that you will be able to put these into practice as you wait for the Lord to return.

DAILY BIBLE DEVOTIONALS

Often, there are no obvious answers to the tensions and troubles of the workplace. What we need is wisdom—God's wisdom. In the book of Proverbs, he provides it.

Day 1

PROVERBS 1:1-7

Q: *What will these proverbs do (v 1-6)?*

Q: *Who are these proverbs for (v 1-6)?*

This is not merely the wisdom of a king (v 1), but of *the* King. Though he did not always live by it, Solomon had been given the wisdom of the Lord (1 Kings 3:5-14). Wisdom is not only specific commands of God—it is general principles to apply to life in all its variety.

Q: *What does real wisdom begin with (Proverbs 1:7)?*

This attitude toward God is the only entrance to true wisdom. It is utterly indispensable. All right understanding and right acting flows from "the fear of the Lord"—a right appreciation and awe of God's character, commands and ways. You will never grow out of needing it, and you will always grow up by heeding it—whether you are "simple" or youthful (just starting out on life, v 4) or "wise" and understanding (further on in living wisely, v 5).

PROVERBS 14:27; 15:33; 22:4

Q: *How do these proverbs give you more motivation to "fear the Lord"?*

PRAY: *Thank God for the proverbs. Pray for wisdom to live and work well.*

Day 2

PROVERBS 6:6-11; 12:24; 20:13; 31:10-18

Q: *How would you sum up the view of work and laziness set out here?*

PROVERBS 21:5

Q: *What do you think is the difference between a "diligent" worker and a "hasty" one? How have you seen this proverb working out in your workplace?*

The Bible commends working hard, but it equally warns against burning out. Over-work is as unwise as under-work. And the antidote to both is the same: the fear of the Lord, so that we approach our tasks remembering that "unless the Lord builds the house, those who build it labor in vain" (Psalm 127:1). We are to labor; but we are always to bear in mind that in all we do, we need the divine Laborer to be at work in, through and around us. And what is the sign that we truly know this? **Read Psalm 127:2.** We don't overwork; we do sleep well.

Q: *How will these proverbs help you live wisely in the practicalities of your work?*

PRAY: *Pray for wisdom to discern any ways in which you are being lazy, or over-working; and for the wisdom to change.*

Day 3

PROVERBS 12:17; 24:26, 28;

Q: *How do these apply in a work context?*

Telling the truth is always the loving thing to do (24:26).

Q: *When is this hardest to believe and live by in your work?*

PROVERBS 12:19-22

Honesty is a way to love our neighbor; it is also a way to love our Lord. Lies are eventually overtaken by the truth (v 19), and lies are remembered and hated by God (v 22).

But it is not only honesty with their lips that characterizes the wise—it is also honesty with their lives. This is what we tend to call integrity.

PROVERBS 10:1, 9; 11:1, 3

Q: *How does integrity guard us (10:9) and guide us (11:3)?*

Living with integrity makes life more relaxed; we do not live looking over our shoulder in fear of being found out in some way. And it makes life simpler: instead of plotting in each situation how to promote or protect ourselves, our career or reputation, we just ask: What's the straight, honest thing to do?

Q: *Is there any way you use "dishonest scales" in your work? What negative effects does this have on you? On your co-workers? On your relationship with God? How will you change?*

PRAY: *Pray you would prize honesty above promoting or protecting yourself.*

Day 4

PROVERBS 10:11; 12:18

Q: *How is the power of words pictured in these two proverbs? What effects can our words have?*

You can likely remember something hurtful someone said to you years ago that caused a scar you still bear. Equally, you may be able to call to mind comments made to you that have caused your feet to skip and your heart to soar. This world was formed by the words of God, and you are made in his image (Genesis 1:3, 26-28). So never underestimate the power of your words: to build up and to tear down, to create joy and to cause dismay.

PROVERBS 15:28

Wisdom ponders before speaking, and then speaks; folly either pours out words without prior reflection—or (an equal and opposite mistake) does not speak when it should.

Q: *Are there situations in your working day where you need to learn to ponder, but tend to pour out?*

PROVERBS 12:25; 15:4; 26:20-22

Q: *How can we use our words, according to these verses? With what differing results?*

Q: *Why is gossip so alluring? How can you introduce positive, godly alternatives when work interactions turn to gossip?*

PRAY: *Read Psalm 12. Thank God that his words are different to the words of the world, and ask that yours might be more like his than the words of those in verses 2-4.*

Day 5

Q: *Do you perform kindnesses for others in the workplace? What prompts those acts?*

PROVERBS 14:31; 19:17

Q: *How do these proverbs link our generosity (or otherwise) to others with our treatment of God?*

Being kind does not only say something about our view of others—it also says something about our view of God. God made everyone in his own image—everyone has intrinsic dignity, and when we mistreat someone else, we show contempt for the One whose image they bear.

Notice that Proverbs 14:31 points us to our treatment of "the needy." It is easy to be kind to those who can repay our kindness—to lend money, time or energy to those who will give us more back. That "kindness" is actually mere self-interest. Wonderfully and counter-intuitively, when we pursue a life of kindness and service, we discover that this is the life of real reward and true blessing (John 13:17).

Godly wisdom is kind because God is kind. The gospel is the declaration that God's kindness appeared (Titus 3:4-7). The gospel moves us to leave self-interest behind (v 3) and live as heirs of God, sharing our Father's character by showing our Father's kindness.

Q: *Who are the "needy"—the non-influential, non-powerful, non-popular ones in your workplace? Are you as kind to them as to those who can repay you?*

PRAY: *Pray for a heart that seeks to be kind, just as the Lord of your heart is kind, motivated by love and not self-interest.*

Day 6

Often, work tensions that involve us do so because we were the ones who ignited or fueled the conflict. But sometimes, we are the victim, rather than the cause, of unfairness or unkindness. What does wisdom look like then?

PROVERBS 12:16; 17:9; 19:11

Q: *How does each show us how to live wisely when offended or insulted?*

Q: *Can you see how each of these wise and unwise responses would look like for you, in your particular work situation?*

PROVERBS 25:21-22

There are often times in our working lives when we spend a large part of our time in close proximity with someone who appears to desire to make our life difficult by treating us unfairly.

Q: *How should we respond? What might this look like in your work environment?*

Verse 22 gives two motivations for the hard work of blessing those who curse us. First, the Lord rewards us in eternity. Second, the start of the verse is likely describing a sign of repentance—as we respond to "dog eat dog" with "dog feed dog," the wrongdoer may admit their fault and seek forgiveness. And it is the gospel that empowers this—for we know that our offense against God is graver than any against us, and his forgiveness and blessing are greater than any that we extend to others.

PRAY: *Reflect on the proverbs you've read. Praise God for ways in which he is already helping you to live wisely; repent where necessary; ask him to change you as you need.*

JOURNAL

What I've learned or been particularly struck by this week…

What I want to change in my perspectives or actions as a result of this week…

Things I would like to think about more or discuss with others at my church…

BIBLE STUDY

Discuss

If someone asked you to sum up the big ideas in *Gospel Shaped Work*, what would you tell them? Which have been the most surprising for you?

Gospel Shaped Work has laid out some powerful ideas that shine a very different light on our working lives, and our understanding as Christians. We've seen that:

- God is revealed as a worker!
- God made us in his image as workers, and that work is good.
- Work has been frustrated by the fall.
- Christ not only redeemed his people through his death and resurrection, but in some way the whole world—our work will be redeemed in the new creation.
- In the new creation, we will continue to be workers—reigning with Christ and extending God's kingdom and glory into the whole of creation.

In Psalm 8, we see some of these key ideas repeated.

☛ READ PSALM 8

> ³ When I look at your heavens, the work of your fingers,
>   the moon and the stars, which you have set in place,
> ⁴ what is man that you are mindful of him,
>   and the son of man that you care for him?

1. Verses 1-3 reveal God as a worker. How do we see the majesty of God's "name" (ie: his reputation) in what he has made?

2. What should these experiences of creation lead us to (v 1, 4)? What do the words used in verse 1 mean and imply?

3. What position has God given to us in the world (v 5-8)? List the honors and responsibilities God has given to humankind.

4. What is the significance of the language used here—"dominion," "crowned," "under [our] feet"? How does v 4-6a help us keep a perspective on this privilege?

5. How should these truths about our nature and position as people in God's world affect the way we view ourselves? How might it change the way we see others?

6. Think about how you feel as you start work on a Monday morning. Think about common attitudes to work among your friends and colleagues. How might the perspective of Psalm 8 change our view of work—whatever that might be?

READ HEBREWS 2:5-9

> [9] *But we see him who for a little while was made lower than the angels, namely Jesus, crowned with glory and honor because of the suffering of death, so that by the grace of God he might taste death for everyone.*

7. The writer quotes Psalm 8. What is his assessment of where humanity as a whole has got to with this command to subdue the earth (see the contrast between v 8b and 8c)?

How has God ultimately fulfilled his own command to humanity (verse 9)?

Apply

FOR YOURSELF: Share with the group one big thing that you have been challenged by during this course. How might you start—and continue—to think and act differently as a result.

FOR YOUR CHURCH: How will you sustain the conversation in your church, and the mutual encouragement about your daily work being part of your godly calling and discipleship? How will you remind each other of the truths we have uncovered during this course?

Pray

FOR YOUR GROUP: Pray through the things that people shared in the Apply section above. Ask the Lord to help them change. But also ask the Lord to help you encourage each other, and remind each other of gospel truths about work when you are ground down by the difficulties and struggles of working in a fallen world.

FOR YOUR CHURCH: Pray that you would be a church that is connected to the world of work in an intelligent and compassionate way, and not a church that is isolated and separate from it. Pray that your church would be a place where all people are honored, respected and encouraged—whatever their work. Pray that the fresh perspectives you have learned in this series would remain alive in your group consciousness.

SERMON NOTES

Bible passage: Date:

GOSPEL SHAPED

CHURCH

The Complete Series

LET THE POWER OF THE GOSPEL SHAPE FOUR OTHER CRITICAL AREAS IN THE LIFE OF YOUR CHURCH

"WE WANT CHURCHES CALLED INTO EXISTENCE BY THE GOSPEL TO BE SHAPED BY THE GOSPEL IN THEIR EVERYDAY LIFE."

DON CARSON AND TIM KELLER

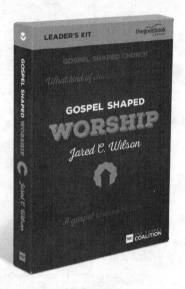

GOSPEL SHAPED
WORSHIP

Christians are people who have discovered that the one true object of our worship is the God who has revealed himself in and through Jesus Christ.

But what exactly is worship? What should we be doing when we meet together for "church" on Sundays? And how does that connect with what we do the rest of the week?

This seven-week whole-church curriculum explores what it means to be a worshiping community. As we search the Scriptures together, we will discover that true worship must encompass the whole of life. This engaging and flexible resource will challenge us to worship God every day of the week, with all our heart, mind, soul and strength.

Written and presented by **JARED C. WILSON**
Jared is Director of Communications at Midwestern Seminary and College in Kansas City, and a prolific author. He is married to Becky and has two daughters.

WWW.GOSPELSHAPEDCHURCH.ORG/WORSHIP

GOSPEL SHAPED
OUTREACH

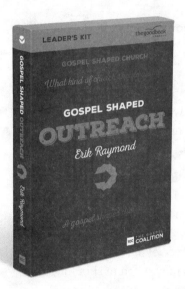

Many Christians are nervous about telling someone else about Jesus. The nine sessions in this curriculum don't offer quick fixes or evangelism "gimmicks." But by continually pointing us back to the gospel, they will give us the proper motivation to work together as a church to share the gospel message with those who are lost without Christ.

As you work through the material, you will discover that God's mission of salvation in the world is also your mission; and that he is inviting you into the privilege of praying and working to advance his kingdom among your family, friends, neighbors, co-workers and community.

Gospel Shaped Church is a new curriculum from The Gospel Coalition that will help whole congregations pause and think slowly, carefully and prayerfully about the kind of church they are called to be.

Written and presented by **ERIK RAYMOND**
Erik is the Preaching Pastor at Emmaus Bible Church in Omaha, Nebraska. He is married to Christie and has six children.

WWW.GOSPELSHAPEDCHURCH.ORG/OUTREACH

GOSPEL SHAPED
LIVING

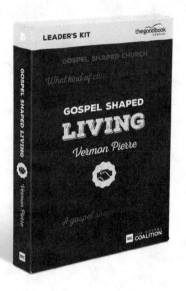

Start a fresh discussion in your church about how the gospel of Christ impacts every area of life in our world.

Gospel Shaped Living is a track that explores over seven sessions what it means for a local church to be a distinctive, counter-cultural community.

Through the gospel, God calls people from every nation, race and background to be joined together in a new family that shows his grace and glory. How should our lives as individuals and as a church reflect and model the new life we have found in Christ? And how different should we be to the world around us?

This challenging and interactive course will inspire us to celebrate grace and let the gospel shape our lives day by day.

Written and presented by **VERMON PIERRE**
Vermon is the Lead Pastor of Roosevelt Community Church in Phoenix, Arizona. He is married to Dennae and has four children.

WWW.GOSPELSHAPEDCHURCH.ORG/LIVING

"THESE RESOURCES GIVE SPACE TO CONSIDER WHAT A GENUINE EXPRESSION OF A GOSPEL-SHAPED CHURCH LOOKS LIKE FOR YOU IN THE PLACE GOD HAS PUT YOU, AND WITH THE PEOPLE HE HAS GATHERED INTO FELLOWSHIP WITH YOU."

DON CARSON AND TIM KELLER

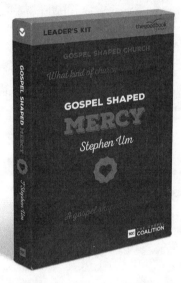

GOSPEL SHAPED
MERCY

The gospel is all about justice and mercy: the just punishment of God falling on his Son, Jesus, so that he can have mercy on me, a sinner.

But many churches have avoided following through on the Bible's clear teaching on working for justice and mercy in the wider world. They fear that it is a distraction from the primary task of gospel preaching.

This *Gospel Shaped Mercy* module explores how individual Christians and whole churches can and should be engaged in the relief of poverty, hunger and injustice in a way that adorns the gospel of grace.

Written and presented by **STEPHEN UM**
Stephen is Senior Minister of Citylife Church in Boston, MA, and is a council member of The Gospel Coalition.

WWW.GOSPELSHAPEDCHURCH.ORG/MERCY

THE GOSPEL
COALITION

This set of resources is based on the five principles of gospel-centered ministry as laid out in The Gospel Coalition's foundation documents. The text reads:

What is gospel–centered ministry?
It is characterized by:

1. Empowered corporate worship

The gospel changes our relationship with God from one of hostility or slavish compliance to one of intimacy and joy. The core dynamic of gospel–centered ministry is therefore worship and fervent prayer. In corporate worship God's people receive a special life–transforming sight of the worth and beauty of God, and then give back to God suitable expressions of his worth. At the heart of corporate worship is the ministry of the Word. Preaching should be expository (explaining the text of Scripture) and Christ–centered (expounding all biblical themes as climaxing in Christ and his work of salvation). Its ultimate goal, however, is not simply to teach but to lead the hearers to worship, individual and corporate, that strengthens their inner being to do the will of God.

2. Evangelistic effectiveness

Because the gospel (unlike religious moralism) produces people who do not disdain those who disagree with them, a truly gospel–centered church should be filled with members who winsomely address people's hopes and aspirations with Christ and his saving work. We have a vision for a church that sees conversions of rich and poor, highly educated and less educated, men and women, old and young, married and single, and all races. We hope to draw highly secular and postmodern people, as well as reaching religious and traditional people. Because of the attractiveness of its community and the humility of its people, a gospel–centered

church should find people in its midst who are exploring and trying to understand Christianity. It must welcome them in hundreds of ways. It will do little to make them "comfortable" but will do much to make its message understandable. In addition to all this, gospel–centered churches will have a bias toward church planting as one of the most effective means of evangelism there is.

3. Counter–cultural community

Because the gospel removes both fear and pride, people should get along inside the church who could never get along outside. Because it points us to a man who died for his enemies, the gospel creates relationships of service rather than of selfishness. Because the gospel calls us to holiness, the people of God live in loving bonds of mutual accountability and discipline. Thus the gospel creates a human community radically different from any society around it. Regarding sex, the church should avoid both the secular society's idolization of sex and traditional society's fear of it. It is a community which so loves and cares practically for its members that biblical chastity makes sense. It teaches its members to conform their bodily being to the shape of the gospel—abstinence outside of heterosexual marriage and fidelity and joy within. Regarding the family, the church should affirm the goodness of marriage between a man and a woman, calling them to serve God by reflecting his covenant love in life–long loyalty, and by teaching his ways to their children. But it also affirms the goodness of serving Christ as singles, whether for a time or for a life. The church should surround all persons suffering from the fallenness of our human sexuality with a compassionate community and family. Regarding money, the church's members should engage in radical economic sharing with one another—so "there are no needy among them" (Acts 4:34). Such sharing also promotes a radically generous commitment of time, money, relationships, and living space to social justice and the needs of the poor, the oppressed, the immigrant, and the economically and physically weak. Regarding power, it is visibly committed to power–sharing and relationship–building among races, classes, and generations that are alienated outside of the Body of Christ. The practical evidence of this is that our local churches increasingly welcome and embrace people of all races and cultures. Each church should seek to reflect the diversity of its local geographical community, both in the congregation at large and in its leadership.

4. The integration of faith and work

The good news of the Bible is not only individual forgiveness but the renewal of the whole creation. God put humanity in the garden to cultivate the material world for his own glory and for the flourishing of nature and the human community. The Spirit of God not only converts individuals (e.g., John 16:8) but also renews and cultivates the face of the earth (e.g., Gen 1:2; Psalm 104:30). Therefore Christians glorify God not only through the ministry of the Word, but also through their vocations of agriculture, art, business, government, scholarship—all for God's glory and the furtherance of the public good. Too many Christians have learned to seal off their faith–beliefs from the way they work in their vocation. The gospel is seen as a means of finding individual peace and not as the foundation of a worldview—a comprehensive interpretation of reality affecting all that we do. But we have a vision for a church that equips its people to think out the implications of the gospel on how we do carpentry, plumbing, data–entry, nursing, art, business, government, journalism, entertainment, and scholarship. Such a church will not only support Christians' engagement with culture, but will also help them work with distinctiveness, excellence, and accountability in their trades and professions. Developing humane yet creative and excellent business environments out of our understanding of the gospel is part of the work of bringing a measure of healing to God's creation in the power of the Spirit. Bringing Christian joy, hope, and truth to embodiment in the arts is also part of this work. We do all of this because the gospel of God leads us to it, even while we recognize that the ultimate restoration of all things awaits the personal and bodily return of our Lord Jesus Christ

5. The doing of justice and mercy

God created both soul and body, and the resurrection of Jesus shows that he is going to redeem both the spiritual and the material. Therefore God is concerned not only for the salvation of souls but also for the relief of poverty, hunger, and injustice. The gospel opens our eyes to the fact that all our wealth (even wealth for which we worked hard) is ultimately an unmerited gift from God. Therefore the person who does not generously give away his or her wealth to others is not merely lacking in compassion, but is unjust. Christ wins our salvation through losing, achieves power through weakness and service, and comes to wealth through giving all away. Those who receive his salvation are not the strong and accomplished but those who admit they are weak and lost. We cannot look at the poor and the oppressed and callously call them to pull themselves out of their own difficulty. Jesus did not treat us that way. The gospel replaces superiority toward the poor with mercy and compassion. Christian churches must work for justice and peace in their neighborhoods through service even as they call individuals to conversion and the new birth. We must work for the eternal and common good and show our neighbors we love them sacrificially whether they believe as we do or not. Indifference to the poor and disadvantaged means there has not been a true grasp of our salvation by sheer grace.

thegoodbook
COMPANY

Opening up the Bible

At The Good Book Company, we are dedicated to helping Christians and local churches grow. We believe that God's growth process always starts with hearing clearly what he has said to us through his timeless word—the Bible.

Ever since we opened our doors in 1991, we have been striving to produce resources that honor God in the way the Bible is used. We have grown to become an international provider of user-friendly resources to the Christian community, with believers of all backgrounds and denominations using our Bible studies, books, evangelistic resources, DVD-based courses and training events.

We want to equip ordinary Christians to live for Christ day by day, and churches to grow in their knowledge of God, their love for one another, and the effectiveness of their outreach.

Call us for a discussion of your needs or visit one of our local websites for more information on the resources and services we provide.

North America: www.thegoodbook.com
UK & Europe: www.thegoodbook.co.uk
Australia: www.thegoodbook.com.au
New Zealand: www.thegoodbook.co.nz

North America: 866 244 2165
UK & Europe: 0333 123 0880
Australia: (02) 6100 4211
New Zealand (+64) 3 343 2463